SALLY MORGAN

THE EASY AIR FRYER COOKBOOK FOR CHILDREN

SCHOLASTIC

TO MY HELPERS, DAISY AND LILY.

Published in the UK, 2025
Scholastic, Bosworth Avenue, Warwick, CV34 6XZ
Scholastic Ireland, 89E Lagan Road, Dublin Industrial Estate, Glasnevin, Dublin, D11 HP5F

SCHOLASTIC and associated logos are trademarks and/or registered trademarks of Scholastic Inc.

Text © Sally Morgan, 2025
Photography © Rachael Crew, 2025
Photographs on pages 26, 29, 43, 61, 63 and 93 © Getty Images, 2025
Photographs on pages 10, 32, 45 and 57 © Shutterstock, 2025
Photographs on page 6 © Getty Images and Shutterstock, 2025

The right of Sally Morgan to be identified as the author of this work has been asserted by her under the Copyright, Designs and Patents Act 1988.

ISBN 978 0702 34232 5

A CIP catalogue record for this book is available from the British Library.

All rights reserved.

This book is sold subject to the condition that it shall not, by way of trade or otherwise, be lent, hired out or otherwise circulated in any form of binding or cover other than that in which it is published. No part of this publication may be reproduced, stored in a retrieval system, or transmitted in any form or by any other means (electronic, mechanical, photocopying, recording or otherwise) or used to train any artificial intelligence technologies without prior written permission of Scholastic Limited.

The recipes in this cookbook contain lots of different ingredients. Some ingredients will not be suitable for everyone, please review all ingredients before cooking to make sure they are suitable for you, your family and your friends and carefully check all food labels.

Scholastic do not have control over the ingredients you use to make these recipes or the environment in which you are making them in. Be aware of cross contamination and always thoroughly clean your preparation area before and after use. Be cautious of hot surfaces and sharp edges when cooking to make sure you, your family and your friends stay safe.

Printed in China

Paper made from wood grown in sustainable forests and other controlled sources.

1 3 5 7 9 10 8 6 4 2

www.scholastic.co.uk

KEY TO THE SYMBOLS IN THIS BOOK:

CONTENTS

INTRODUCTION 4

SPRING

Egg Blossoms	8
Welsh Rarebit	9
Scotch Eggs	10
Spring Onion Soda Bread	12
Smoked Salmon Loaded Potato Skins	14
Vegetable Pakora	16
Carrot Cupcakes	18
Baklava Parcels	20
Red Velvet Cupcakes	22
Chocolate Orange Bread Puddings	24
Easter Egg Cookies	26

SUMMER

Herby Potato Salad	28
Super Simple Flatbreads	29
Hot Honey Chicken Strips	30
Prawn Scampi	32
Crispy 'Crab' Snacks	33
Halloumi Mini Skewers	34
Avocado Dippers	36
Ham and Cheese Quiche	38
Falafel Pitta Pockets	40
Lamb Shish Kebabs	42
Roasted Cauliflower Steaks	44
Caramelized Pineapple	46
Chocolate Marshmallow Fondue	47
Strawberries and Cream Butterfly Cakes	48
Jammy French Toast Roll-ups	50
Air-fried Alaska	52

AUTUMN

Pumpkin Soup	54
Chicken Tikka Bites	56
Masala-spiced Nuts	58
Cheese Mummies	59
Garlic-stuffed Mushrooms	60
Pumpkin-spiced Granola	62
Spring Green Matcha Biscuits	64
Parkin Mini Loaf	65
Spiced Apple Cake	66
Chocolate Chip Catherine Wheels	68
Firecracker Biscuits	70
Stone-fruit Crumbles	72

WINTER

Turkey Burgers	74
Cranberry and Orange Stuffing Balls	76
Parsnip Chips	78
Sweet and Sour Meatballs	80
Crispy Sesame Beef	82
Cheesy Artichoke Fondue	84
Winter Berry Breakfast Oats	86
Sticky Toffee Pudding	88
Snowy Fir Trees	90
Peppermint Swirls	92
Festive Pasties	94

INDEX 96

INTRODUCTION

Feeling hungry and have an air fryer? Well, I have some good (and some bad) news for you! The good news is that with this book, you are just minutes away from enjoying 50 delicious, easy-to-air-fry treats as well as tips for cheffing up your dishes.

'But wait, what's the bad news?' I hear you ask. The bad news is that because all 50 of the recipes in this book are EASY TO MAKE, EASY TO FOLLOW and only require ingredients that are EASY TO FIND, you are going to find it very HARD TO DECIDE which one to try first. So, what are you waiting for? Get started now!

WHY AIR FRY?

IT'S EASY
Set the temperature and the timer and let the air fryer do the rest.

IT'S SPEEDY
Air fryers cook food quickly by blasting it with hot air propelled by powerful fans.

IT'S HEALTHY
Air fryers use a lot less oil than traditional oil frying, so you can recreate some of your favourite fried foods using a lot less fat.

IT'S ECO-FRIENDLY
Air fryers use less electricity than conventional ovens because they are smaller and cook more quickly.

IT'S LESS MESSY
Air fryers and their accessories are easy to clean compared to bulky oven trays or greasy oil-fryer baskets. Just soak the basket or rack in hot water with washing-up liquid while you enjoy your food!

IT'S SAFE
Provided that you follow the safety instructions that come with your air fryer, air frying is much safer than traditional oil frying.

HOW DO AIR FRYERS WORK?

An air fryer cooks food by circulating hot air around it using a fan. The hot air crisps and browns the food without having to dunk it in hot oil. Air fryer baskets and trays contain holes that allow the air to move around the food quickly, cooking it from all sides.

What type of fryer do you have?

AIR FRYER OVEN
Does your air fryer have a door that you can open with removable racks and trays inside? This is an air fryer oven. Air fryer ovens tend to be larger than cylindrical basket-type air fryers and may have more functions such as toast, dehydrate, roast and steam. For the recipes in this book you will only need to use the air-fry function of your oven. The trays and or baskets inside your air fryer oven get very hot. Make sure to always use oven gloves or tongs when attempting to remove them from your fryer.

BASKET AIR FRYERS
Does your air fryer have a drawer with a handle that you can use to remove it from the fryer? This is a basket air fryer. Basket air fryers tend to be smaller than air fryer ovens, but that means they take up less space on your worktop. The handle of the fryer basket makes it easy to remove, so that you can turn the food without having to touch hot surfaces.

All the recipes contained in this book have been tested in both an air fryer oven and a basket air fryer, which means you will be able to make the recipes no matter which type you have; however, it is very important to read the manual that came with your air fryer.

Every model of air fryer is a bit different. The instructions in the manual will give you specific information on how to use your air fryer safely. The manual will also give you useful tips on how to get the best results from your fryer, such as how long it takes the air fryer to preheat, and how to clean it, so it's ready to go next time.

A GUIDE TO SAFE AIR FRYING

BEFORE FRYING

- Always check with a responsible adult before using your air fryer.
- Make sure your air fryer is clean and is sitting on a stable, flat surface.
- Read the recipe through first to make sure you have everything you need.
- Gather and prepare the ingredients and equipment you are going to need.
- Ask for help if you need it!

WHILE FRYING

- Make sure to always use oven gloves and tongs when touching hot surfaces and food inside your fryer.
- Don't be a stranger! Check in on your food while it is cooking.
- Never put air fryer paper liners inside the fryer basket during the preheating stage or without food on top of them.

AFTER FRYING

- Be really careful when removing hot food or baking dishes from the air fryer. Always use oven gloves or tongs, and ask an adult to help if you need it.
- Make sure that food cooked inside the air fryer is piping hot right through.
- Do not eat food straight out of the fryer. IT'S HOT! Leave it to cool for 5–10 minutes.

TIPS FOR SUCCESSFUL AIR FRYING

WATCH THE TIME
The recipes in this book suggest how long your food will take to cook, but all air fryers are different. Some air fryers cook quickly while others may take a bit longer. To ensure you get the best results from your air fryer, make sure to check on your food while it is cooking.

GIVE IT SOME SPACE
Take care not to overfill your fryer. Air fryers cook food by surrounding it with hot air. Crowding the fryer basket stops the air from moving around the food and prevents it from cooking evenly.

MANAGE YOUR EXPECTATIONS
Air fryers are great, but they don't get the same results as traditional frying. Foods cooked in the air fryer may not get quite as crisp and golden as fried foods, but they are just as delicious.

AIR-FRYING EQUIPMENT

Air fryers don't need lots of fancy accessories to make delicious food, but here is a list of a few useful tools that make air frying easier, safer and much more fun!

OIL SPRAY
Air fryers can cook your food without oil, but spritzing some foods with a little oil before air frying helps them to become crisp and golden.

THERMOMETER
If you don't already have one, a digital meat or probe thermometer is a useful, potentially lifesaving tool in the kitchen.

Raw foods such as meat and poultry can contain harmful bacteria that can make you very unwell. Cooking food to a high temperature kills bacteria and makes the food safe to eat. When air frying, it is important to make sure that your food is cooked all the way through and that the heat from the air fryer has made it to the middle of the piece of food. Using a meat thermometer is a quick and easy way to be sure that your food is piping hot all the way through and safe to eat.

These thermometers can be found in kitchen shops or online.

SILICONE CUPCAKE CASES
Silicone is good for air frying because it can withstand high temperatures and is easy to clean. Reusable silicone cupcake cases come in lots of bright colours and are perfect for making small batches of cakes and muffins. Unlike paper, silicone cupcake cases are strong enough to use without a baking tin.

RAMEKINS
The recipes in this book have been created for ramekins that are 9 cm in diameter and 5 cm deep, or roughly 200 ml capacity. If you have different sized ramekins, you will need to adjust the cooking temperature and time.

TONGS
Everyone knows that if you touch things that are very hot, you will get burned. Stop this from happening by making sure you do not touch the inside of your fryer or anything that has just come out of the fryer using your bare hands. Always use tongs to put food into the hot air fryer, to turn it or move it inside the basket and to remove it from the fryer.

OVEN GLOVES
Tongs are great for picking up small pieces of food, but bigger things, such as egg moulds or ramekins, can be more difficult. A good pair of oven gloves, or a single glove, alongside tongs in your other hand should make it easy to get food out of the fryer.

AIR FRYER LINERS
Air fryer liners can be made out of greaseproof paper or silicone. Liners stop foods from sticking to the inside of your fryer. Air fryer liners are pre-cut to the size of your air fryer basket. Paper liners may also have small holes cut in to allow air to circulate throughout the fryer and crisp the food. Some paper liners don't have holes in them, but these are fine to use too, you just might need to turn the food over during the cooking process.

Only use air fryer paper liners with food on top of them. Never use paper liners when preheating your air fryer as they can fly around the basket and catch fire.

HEATPROOF MAT
Never put anything that has just come out of your air fryer on to your worktop. Always place on a plate or a heatproof mat. Heatproof mats are made from plastic, fabric or wood and will protect your worktop from burning or melting.

That's about it. All that's left now is to choose what you want to make first. Turkey burgers? Vegetable pakoras? Caramelized pineapple? Check with an adult, gather all of the ingredients and gear you need, and get cooking!

SPRING

EGG BLOSSOMS

MAKES 2 EGG BLOSSOMS | TAKES 10 MINUTES

This quick and simple recipe will turn your breakfast into a tasty spring bouquet!

INGREDIENTS:

1 medium pepper (or 2 peppers if you want two different coloured flowers)

2 medium eggs

Oil spray

1 spring onion, chopped

CHEF IT UP!
How about a blooming omelette? Whisk your egg in a bowl and add a tablespoon of grated cheese or chopped ham. Pour the mixture into the pepper slice and cook as before. Yum!

1. Preheat the air fryer to 200°C/400°F for 5 minutes.
2. To make your pepper egg rings, use a sharp knife to carefully cut two 2-cm-thick slices from your pepper.
3. Scrape out any seeds and white pith from the inside of your rings using a spoon.
4. Spray the inside of your cooking tray with oil.
5. Place the rings on the tray. Make sure the slices sit flat with no gaps.
6. Crack an egg into each ring.
7. Carefully lower the tray into the air fryer.
8. Set the temperature to 200°C/400°F and the timer for 3 minutes.
9. When the time is up, open the fryer. The egg white should be cooked all the way through with only a little wobble.
10. If your eggs don't look as done as you would like, close the fryer and cook for another minute before checking again.
11. Carefully lift the tray out of the fryer using tongs or oven gloves and place on a heatproof mat.
12. Slide the eggs off the tray using a spatula. Serve by themselves or on a slice of buttered toast. Sprinkle on some chopped spring onions for the finishing touch.

WELSH RAREBIT

SERVES 1 | TAKES 15 MINUTES

Make this quick and cheesy recipe the next time you want a hot snack in a hurry.

INGREDIENTS:

1 thick slice of bread

70 g cheddar, grated

2 tbsp milk

½ tsp cider vinegar

1 tsp Worcestershire sauce

½ tsp mustard powder

½ tsp ground black pepper

1. Put the slice of bread into the air fryer basket. Set the temperature to 200°C/390°F and the timer for 3 minutes.
2. When the time is up, use tongs to turn the slice of bread over. Set the temperature to 200°C/390°F and the timer for 2 minutes.
3. Add the cheese, milk, cider vinegar, Worcestershire sauce, mustard and pepper to a small bowl and mix together with a spoon.
4. When the time is up, open the fryer, the bread should look golden and toasted.
5. Carefully remove the toast from the fryer using tongs and put it on a plate.
6. Spoon the cheese mixture on to the toasted bread. Use the back of the spoon to spread the mixture evenly, making sure it goes right up to the edges.
7. Carefully put the cheese-covered bread into the air fryer basket, cheese side up. Set the temperature to 180°C/360°F and the timer for 6 minutes.
8. When the time is up, open the fryer. The cheese should have melted into the mixture and look bubbling and golden brown. If it doesn't look as cooked as you would like, cook for another minute before checking again.
9. Carefully remove the rarebit from the fryer using tongs or a spatula and serve with a crunchy salad.

CHEF IT UP!

Transform a savoury snack lunch into a hearty dinner by adding a fried egg on top!

SCOTCH EGGS

MAKES 4 SCOTCH EGGS | TAKES 45 MINUTES

Crunchy breadcrumbs, savoury sausage and yummy egg. Delicious served hot or cold, Scotch eggs are a family favourite. Make some for your next family picnic.

INGREDIENTS:

- 5 medium eggs
- 400 g sausage meat
- ½ tsp dried sage
- ½ tsp dried thyme
- ½ tsp salt
- ½ tsp ground black pepper
- 100 g dried breadcrumbs
- 4 tbsp flour
- Oil spray

1. Fill a medium saucepan with water and place it on the hob. Heat the water over a high heat until it starts to boil. Use a spoon to lower four eggs (save one egg for later) into the boiling water, one at a time. Set a timer for 7 minutes.

2. Fill a large bowl with water and add roughly a dozen ice cubes. When the time is up, carefully remove the eggs from the saucepan using a spoon and place them in the iced water. Leave the eggs in the water until they have completely cooled.

3. While the eggs are cooling, add the sausage meat to a medium bowl. Add the herbs, salt, pepper and 2 tbsp of the breadcrumbs. Mix the ingredients together using a spoon. You may need to use your hands to bring the mixture together.

4. When the eggs have cooled, crack the shell of one egg by tapping it against the worktop or the side of the bowl of water. Put the egg back in the water and carefully peel away the cracked shell using your thumb. Continue peeling the shell from the egg until there is none left. Remove the peeled egg from the water and put it on a piece of kitchen roll. Repeat this for the three remaining eggs.

5. Pat the eggs dry with kitchen roll. Tip the flour onto a plate. Place the eggs into the flour and roll them around until they are well coated.

6. Place a piece of cling film on your worktop. Divide the sausage mixture into four equally sized balls. Place a ball of sausage meat onto the cling film. Place another piece of cling film on top. Use a rolling pin to flatten the sausage meat between the two pieces of cling film until it is about 1 cm thick and roughly 12–15 cm in diameter.

7. Remove the top piece of cling film and place one floured egg in the middle. Pick up the cling film with the sausage and egg on top. Wrap the egg in the sausage meat by cupping the cling film around the egg. Smooth the sausage meat around the egg until the egg is covered completely. Use your fingers to help. Try to make sure your layer of sausage meat is as even as possible around the egg and that there are no air pockets. An uneven coating or air pockets can cause the sausage meat to crack while cooking, but don't worry, even if it does crack a little, your Scotch egg will still taste delicious!

8. When the egg is covered, remove it from the cling film and put it onto the plate with the flour.

9. Reuse the pieces of cling film to cover the remaining three eggs with the balls of sausage meat. Roll each sausage-covered egg in the flour.

10. Crack the remaining egg into a medium bowl and beat it with a fork. Tip the breadcrumbs onto a plate.

11. Preheat the air fryer to 200°C/390°F for 5 minutes.

12. Roll each sausage- and flour-covered egg in the bowl with the beaten egg and then in the breadcrumbs. The egg will help the breadcrumbs to stick. Place the eggs on a piece of kitchen roll.

13. Spray the eggs with a little oil and then carefully place them in the hot air fryer basket using tongs. Set the temperature to 200°C/390°F and the timer for 7 minutes.

14. When the time is up, open the fryer and turn the eggs over using tongs. Set the temperature to 200°C/390°F and the timer for 7 minutes.

15. When the time is up, open the fryer. The breadcrumbs should look crisp and golden brown.

16. Carefully remove the eggs from the fryer using tongs. Serve hot or cold with your favourite sauce.

CHEF IT UP!
Try adding some grated parmesan cheese to your breadcrumbs for a cheesy crispy crust!

SPRING ONION SODA BREAD

MAKES 1 LOAF | TAKES 60 MINUTES

This hearty loaf is easy to make and delicious served with soup or your favourite eggs.

INGREDIENTS:

500 g wholemeal flour

1 ½ tsp salt

1 ½ tsp bicarbonate of soda

70 g cheddar, grated

4 spring onions, chopped

450 ml buttermilk

1. Combine the flour, salt and bicarbonate of soda in a large bowl and mix well.
2. Add the cheese and the spring onions and stir.
3. Stir in one third of the buttermilk.
4. Add another third of the buttermilk and stir again. You may want to use your hands to bring the dough together.
5. Add the rest of the buttermilk a little at a time, bringing the dry and wet ingredients together with your hands until there are no dry bits in the bowl. The dough will be sticky and rough looking.
6. Dust your hands with a little flour, then shape your dough into a round loaf shape approximately 20 cm across. Place the loaf on a paper liner.
7. Use a sharp knife to cut a 3-cm deep cross into the top of your loaf. This will help the heat to reach the centre.
8. Preheat your air fryer to 160°C/320°F for 5 minutes.
9. Carefully put the paper liner with your loaf into the basket of the air fryer.
10. Set the temperature to 160°C/320°F and the timer for 50 minutes.
11. When the time is up, use a spatula or clean oven gloves to carefully remove the loaf from the fryer. The loaf should look brown and crispy on top. Turn the loaf over and tap it with your fingers. A cooked loaf will make a hollow sound.
12. If the loaf does not sound hollow, or doesn't look as cooked as you would like, put it back into the fryer and cook at 160°C/320°F for 5 minutes.
13. Let the loaf cool on a rack. Serve with soup or simply with lots of butter.

SMOKED SALMON LOADED POTATO SKINS

MAKES 8 POTATO SKINS | TAKES 1 HOUR 20 MINUTES

These crispy potato bites make a delicious snack, but look elegant enough to serve as starter for a special meal or even a fancy canapé for a party.

INGREDIENTS:

4 medium-sized potatoes, cleaned

2 tbsp olive oil

2 tsp salt

2 tsp ground black pepper

200 g cream cheese

4 tbsp soured cream

1 tbsp lemon juice

100 g smoked salmon, chopped

2 tbsp fresh dill or chives, chopped, plus a little extra to garnish

Oil spray

CHEF IT UP!
Salmon not your thing? Stuff the potatoes with any filling of your choice. Tuna mayo is delicious.

1. Preheat the air fryer to 200°C/400°F for 5 minutes.

2. Add the potatoes, 1 tbsp of olive oil and ½ tsp of salt and pepper to a large bowl. Toss the potatoes in the olive oil and seasonings until they are well coated.

3. Use tongs to carefully place the potatoes in the air fryer basket. Set the temperature to 200°C/400°F and the timer for 30 minutes.

4. To make the filling, add the cream cheese, soured cream, lemon juice and ½ tsp of salt and pepper to a medium bowl. Mix together with a fork. You can use an electric whisk if you have one. Mix until they are well combined.

5. Add the smoked salmon and the herbs and mix in gently with a fork. Cover the bowl and put it in the fridge.

6. When the time is up, open the fryer. The potatoes should look crispy on the outside. To check if they are cooked, push the blade of a table knife into the centre of one potato. Once through the crispy skin, the inside of the potato should feel soft and not crunchy or hard beneath the blade. If the potatoes are not as done as you would like, cook for another 2–3 minutes before checking again.

7. Remove the potatoes from the fryer and leave them to cool for 15–20 minutes.

8. Preheat the air fryer to 200°C/400°F for 5 minutes.

9. Once the potatoes are cool enough to handle, use a sharp knife to carefully cut each potato in half.

10. Use a teaspoon to scoop out some of the potato from each half to make the potatoes into little cups. Try to leave a 1-cm-thick layer of potato inside each half. You can save the removed potato flesh to use in another recipe (see Vegetable Pakoras on page 16).

11. Spray the insides of the potato skins with a little oil and sprinkle over a little more salt and pepper. Use tongs to arrange the potato skins in the air fryer basket. Try to leave a bit of space around each one. You may need to work in batches.

12. Set the temperature to 200°C/400°F and the timer for 10 minutes.

13. When the time is up, the insides of the potatoes should look crisp and a little brown around the edges. If they don't look as crispy as you would like, cook for another 2–3 minutes before checking again.

14. Remove the potatoes from the fryer using tongs and leave them to cool. If you are serving the potato skins right away, they only need to cool for 4–5 minutes before you fill them. If you are serving the potato skins cold, let them cool completely before adding your filling.

15. Take the bowl with the filling out of the fridge and uncover it.

16. Use a teaspoon to scoop a generous dollop of the filling from the bowl. Use another teaspoon to scrape the filling into the first potato skin. Repeat this until all of the skins are filled. Some may need more than one teaspoon. Save any extra filling to serve on the side, for people to add themselves.

17. Top each potato skin with a sprinkle of chopped chives or a sprig of dill.

VEGETABLE PAKORA

MAKES 6-8 PAKORAS | TAKES 25 MINUTES

Transform leftover mashed potato to crunchy vegetable bites packed with flavour.

INGREDIENTS:

½ medium onion, sliced thinly

¼ tsp salt

40 g cauliflower

½ tsp ground turmeric

1 tsp grated ginger

½ tsp ground black pepper

½ tsp garam masala

¼ tsp chilli powder

200 g mashed potato (why not use left overs from the Loaded Potato Skins recipe on page 14?)

2 tbsp chopped coriander

30 g gram (chickpea) flour

Oil spray

TO SERVE:

4 tbsp mango chutney

1. Add the sliced onions and salt to a medium bowl and mix together with spoon.
2. Crumble in the cauliflower and add the turmeric, grated ginger, garam masala and chilli powder. Mix together well.
3. Preheat the air fryer to 200°C/390°F for 5 minutes.
4. Add the mashed potato, coriander and gram flour to the bowl and mix. You may need to use your hands. If the mixture is a little dry, add 1 tbsp of water and mix.
5. Take a handful of mixture and form it into a patty measuring about 5 cm across and 2 cm thick. Put the patty onto a plate.
6. Repeat step 5 with the rest of the mixture.
7. Spray the each of patties with a little oil.
8. Spray the inside of your air fryer basket with a little oil. Use a spatula to carefully place the patties into the air fryer basket. Leave some space around each patty. You may need to work in batches depending on the size of your fryer.
9. Set the temperature to 200°C/390°F and the timer for 4 minutes.
10. When the time is up, use a spatula to carefully turn over each patty. Set the temperature to 200°C/390°F and the timer for 4 minutes.
11. When the time is up, open the fryer. The pakoras should look golden and crisp around the edges. If they don't look as done as you would like, cook for another 1–2 minutes before checking again.
12. Use a spatula or tongs to remove the patties from the fryer.
13. Serve hot with mango chutney on the side.

SPRING

CARROT CUPCAKES

MAKES 8–12 CUPCAKES | TAKES 40 MINUTES

These carroty cupcakes make a super-delicious springtime dessert or snack.

INGREDIENTS:

100 g plain flour

1 tsp baking powder

½ tsp ground cinnamon

100 g brown sugar

1 tsp orange zest

½ tsp salt

1 egg, beaten

1 tbsp orange juice

80 ml vegetable oil

1 tsp vanilla extract

100 g carrot, grated

50 g raisins

30 g walnuts, chopped

FOR THE ICING:

30 g cream cheese

30 g butter, softened

100 g icing sugar

1 tsp orange juice

Some candied orange peel or few extra walnut halves to decorate

EQUIPMENT:

Electric whisk

CHEF IT UP! Give these cupcakes a real springtime twist by replacing the walnut with one of your favourite chocolate eggs.

1. Preheat the air fryer to 160°C/320°F for 5 minutes.
2. Add the flour, baking powder, cinnamon, brown sugar, orange zest and salt to a medium bowl. Stir the ingredients together with a spoon.
3. Add the egg, orange juice, vegetable oil and vanilla extract to a second bowl and beat them together with a fork.
4. Pour the egg mixture into the flour mixture and stir using a spoon until the mixture has combined.
5. Stir in the grated carrot, raisins and walnuts.
6. Spoon the mixture into the cupcake cases until they are three-quarters full.
7. Carefully place the cupcake cases into the hot air fryer basket using tongs.
8. Set the temperature to 160°C/325°F and the timer for 12 minutes.

9 When the time is up, open the fryer. The cupcakes should look risen and golden. To check if they are cooked, push a metal skewer or the blade of a table knife into the centre of one cupcake and pull it out. The blade should come out clean with only a few crumbs clinging to it. If the blade comes out with raw mixture on it, close the fryer and cook for another 2–3 minutes before checking again.

10 Carefully remove the cupcakes from the fryer using tongs and place them on a wire cooling rack.

11 To make the icing, add the icing sugar, cream cheese, butter and orange juice to a medium bowl. Use an electric whisk to beat the ingredients together until fluffy and smooth. Put the icing in the fridge until the cakes have completely cooled.

12 When the cupcakes have cooled, spoon 1 tbsp of icing on to the top of each cupcake. Spread out the icing using a table knife.

13 Place a few strips of candied orange peel or a walnut half on top of each cupcake.

Warning! This recipe contains nuts. Make sure none of your family or friends have nut allergies before sharing these cupcakes with them.

SPRING

BAKLAVA PARCELS

MAKES 12 PARCELS | TAKES 45 MINUTES

Crisp, bite-sized pastry parcels filled with honey-soaked nuts.

INGREDIENTS:

40 g dried breadcrumbs

½ tsp salt

100 g melted butter

6 tbsp honey

50 g pistachio nuts, chopped

50 g walnuts, chopped

200 g filo pastry (6 large sheets from a pack)

EQUIPMENT:

12-hole muffin tin

Pastry brush

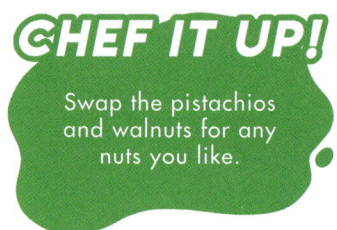

CHEF IT UP! Swap the pistachios and walnuts for any nuts you like.

1. Add the breadcrumbs, salt, 3 tbsp of the melted butter and 4 tbsp of the honey to a small bowl and mix together using a spoon. Add most of the chopped nuts, saving some to garnish at the end. Put the bowl to one side.

2. Use a pastry brush to lightly grease the cups of a 12-hole muffin tin with melted butter. Don't worry if your tin is too big for your air fryer, it will only be used to shape your parcels.

3. Unroll the filo pastry and place 6 sheets on a clean, dry work surface, laid on top of each other. Use a sharp knife to carefully cut the pastry into 6 squares, measuring roughly 12 cm by 12 cm. This should make 36 squares altogether. Cover the pastry with a piece of damp kitchen roll or a damp tea towel until you are ready to use it.

4. Take 1 square of pastry and lay it on your work surface. Use the pastry brush to brush the pastry with butter.

5. Take another square of pastry and lay it on top of the first, so that it makes a star shape. Brush this square with butter, before laying on a third square.

6. Carefully pick up the pastry and place it on top of one cup of the muffin tin. Carefully push the centre of the pastry into the tin.

7. Spoon 1–2 tbsps of the nut mixture into the centre of the pastry cup. Dip your fingers in a little water and use them to moisten the pastry above the filling. Pinch the pastry together to make a parcel.

8. Repeat steps 4–7 with the rest of your pastry squares. Put any remaining filling to one side. Remember to recover the remaining pastry with the damp kitchen roll, as you work, to stop it from drying out.

9. Preheat the air fryer to 160°C/325°F for 5 minutes.

10. When the fryer is hot, use tongs to remove the parcels from the muffin tin and carefully place them in the fryer basket. Leave some space around each parcel. You may need to work in batches. Set the temperature to 160°C/325°F and the timer for 12 minutes.

11 When the time is up, open the fryer. The parcels should look crisp and golden and even a little brown at the edges. If the parcels don't look as done as you would like, close the fryer and cook for another 2–3 minutes before checking again.

12 Use tongs to carefully remove the parcels from the basket and put them on a plate. Drizzle the parcels with the remaining honey and sprinkle over the reserved nuts and any remaining filling.
Leave the parcels to cool for at least 5 minutes before enjoying!

Warning! This recipe contains nuts. Make sure none of your family or friends have nut allergies before sharing these baklava parcels with them.

RED VELVET CUPCAKES

MAKES 8–10 CUPCAKES | TAKES 30 MINUTES

Make a luxurious Valentine's treat for the people you love with these choco-vanilla cupcakes.

SPRING

INGREDIENTS:

80 g plain flour

1 tsp cocoa powder

¼ tsp bicarbonate of soda

80 g caster sugar

60 g butter, melted

1 tsp vanilla extract

60 ml milk

1 egg

1 tsp white vinegar or apple cider vinegar

1 tsp red food colouring

FOR THE ICING:

100 g icing sugar

30 g cream cheese

30 g butter, softened

1 tsp milk

TO DECORATE:

4 tbsp sprinkles

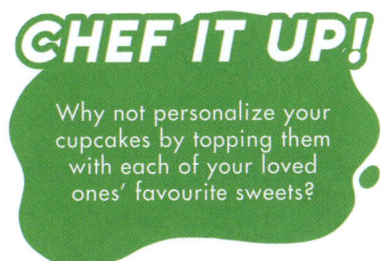

CHEF IT UP! Why not personalize your cupcakes by topping them with each of your loved ones' favourite sweets?

1. Preheat the air fryer to 150°C/300°F for 5 minutes.
2. Add the flour, cocoa powder and bicarbonate of soda to a medium bowl and stir well to combine.
3. Add the sugar, melted butter, vanilla extract, milk, egg and vinegar to another medium bowl and beat together using a wooden spoon or an electric whisk. Mix together until all the ingredients are well combined.
4. Add one third of the flour and cocoa mixture to the wet ingredients and mix until you can't see any flour. Add half of the rest of the flour and cocoa and mix again. Repeat until all of the dry ingredients have been mixed into the wet ingredients.
5. Add a few drops of red food colouring to the mixture and stir. If the mixture looks only a little pink after stirring in the food colouring, add a few more drops before stirring again. Keep adding drops of food colouring to your mixture until it is a vibrant red colour.
6. Spoon the mixture into the silicone cupcake cases. Fill each case until it is about three-quarters full.
7. Set the temperature to 150°C/300°F and the timer for 10 minutes.
8. When the time is up, open the fryer. The cupcakes should have risen and look dry on top. To check if they are cooked, push the blade of a table knife into the centre of one cupcake. If the blade comes out clean with only a few crumbs clinging to it, the cupcakes are ready. If the blade comes out with wet mixture on it, or the cupcakes don't look as done as you would like, cook for another 2–3 minutes before checking again.
9. Remove the cupcakes from the fryer using tongs and leave them to cool on a cooling rack.
10. To make the icing, add the icing sugar, cream cheese, butter and milk to a medium bowl. Use an electric whisk to beat the ingredients together until fluffy and smooth. Put the icing in the fridge until the cakes have completely cooled.
11. When the cupcakes have cooled, spoon 1 tbsp of icing on the top of each cupcake. Spread the icing out using a table knife.
12. Tip the sprinkles into a shallow dish. Dip the top of each cupcake into the dish of sprinkles.

CHOCOLATE ORANGE BREAD PUDDINGS

MAKES 2 BREAD PUDDINGS | TAKES 25 MINUTES

This rich dessert is the perfect way to round off a meal.

INGREDIENTS:

Butter, for greasing

2 eggs

200 ml milk

30 g caster sugar

1 tsp vanilla extract

1 tsp grated orange zest

30 g chocolate chips

120 g stale white bread, cut into cubes

EQUIPMENT:

2 ramekins

1. Prepare the ramekins by dipping a piece of kitchen roll in butter and rubbing it around the inside of each pot until they are evenly coated in butter.

2. Crack the eggs into a jug and whisk with a fork. Add the milk, sugar, vanilla extract and orange zest to the bowl and whisk together until all the sugar has dissolved.

3. Arrange a layer of bread cubes in the bottom of each ramekin and sprinkle over some of the chocolate chips.

4. Pour enough of the egg mixture into each ramekin to cover the cubes.

5. Add the remaining cubes of bread and chocolate chips on top. Press gently on the bread cubes to help them absorb the mixture.

6. Pour over the remaining mixture to fill the ramekins. Don't fill them right to the top as the bread puddings will rise a bit.

7. Preheat the air fryer to 160°C/325°F for 5 minutes.

8. Use tongs or oven gloves to carefully place the ramekins into the air fryer basket. Set the temperature to 160°C/325°F and the timer for 10 minutes.

9. When the time is up, open the air fryer. The puddings should look crisp and golden on top. To check they are cooked through, push a knife into the middle of one pudding and pull it out. If the knife comes out clean with no wet mixture on it, the puddings are ready. If the knife comes out with wet mixture clinging to it, cook for 2–3 minutes before checking again.

10. Carefully remove the puddings from the fryer using tongs or oven gloves and leave to cool for 5 minutes before serving.

CHEF IT UP!

Experiment with different flavours. Replace the chocolate chips with raisins or other dried fruit or why not try using leftover tea cakes or hot cross buns instead of bread?

EASTER EGG COOKIES

MAKES 15-18 COOKIES | TAKES 30 MINUTES

This chocolate egg twist on traditional chocolate chip cookies makes a delicious and pretty springtime treat!

INGREDIENTS:

80 g chocolate mini eggs

100 g butter, melted

80 g caster sugar

½ tsp salt

½ tsp vanilla extract

200 g plain flour

1 medium egg

1. Put the mini eggs into a plastic food bag. Use a rolling pin to crack and break up the mini eggs by tapping the outside of the bag. Do not totally crush the mini eggs as you want some nice big pieces.

2. Preheat the air fryer to 160°C/325°F for 5 minutes.

3. Add the melted butter, sugar, salt and vanilla extract to a large bowl and mix with a wooden spoon.

4. Add the flour and the egg and mix until you have a thick, sticky dough.

5. Add three-quarters of the broken mini eggs and stir gently until they are mixed evenly into the mixture.

6. Place a paper liner on your worktop. Scoop 1 heaped tbsp of cookie dough from the bowl and scrape it off the spoon onto the paper liner. Squash the blob of dough slightly with the back of a spoon. Press a pinch of the reserved broken mini eggs into each cookie. You don't need to flatten it completely as the cookies will spread while they bake.

7. Scoop another tablespoon of dough out of the bowl and scrape it onto the liner 4–5 cm from the first, and squash it with the back of your spoon. Add a pinch of the reserved broken mini eggs to each cookie. Repeat this until your liner is covered with blobs of dough. You may have to bake the cookies in batches.

8. Remove the basket from your air fryer and carefully place the liner inside.

9. Put the basket back into the fryer. Set the temperature to 160°C/325°F and the timer for 12 minutes.

10. When the time is up, open the fryer and look at your cookies. If they have spread out and look a little dry on top, leave the air fryer basket on a heatproof mat or carefully remove the liner from the fryer and place it on a cooling rack. If they still look quite doughy, cook them for 1–2 minutes before checking again.

11. Leave the cookies to cool for 10 minutes before serving.

SPRING

SUMMER

HERBY HOT POTATO SALAD

MAKES 4 SIDE PORTIONS | TAKES 35 MINUTES

This hot summer salad is delicious served with barbecued meat or fish. Choose dill, parsley, oregano or any herbs you like.

INGREDIENTS:

2 tbsp olive oil

1 tsp salt

1 tsp ground black pepper

1 tsp paprika

800 g potatoes, scrubbed and cut into 3-cm cubes

½ medium onion, chopped

100 g feta cheese, crumbled

1 tbsp lemon juice

3 tbsp fresh herbs, chopped

1. Preheat the air fryer to 200°C/400°F for 5 minutes.
2. Add the olive oil, salt, pepper and paprika to a large bowl and mix well with a spoon.
3. Add the cubed potatoes to the bowl. Toss the potatoes in the oil and spice mixture until they are well coated.
4. Tip the potatoes into the air fryer basket.
5. Set the temperature to 200°C/400°F and the timer for 12 minutes.
6. When the time is up, open the air fryer. Add the chopped onions to the basket and toss with the potatoes using tongs.
7. Set the temperature to 200°C/400°F and the timer for 7 minutes.
8. When the time is up, the potatoes should look golden brown and the onions soft. Check the potatoes by pushing a fork into one potato. The fork should slide into the potato easily. If the potatoes are a bit hard or don't look as crispy as you would like, cook at 200°C/400°F for another 3 minutes before checking again.
9. When the potatoes are cooked, tip them into a large bowl. Add the lemon juice, herbs and feta cheese. Toss the ingredients together using tongs.

(VG) (VE)

SUPER-SIMPLE FLATBREADS

MAKES 4 FLATBREADS | TAKES 20 MINUTES

These flatbreads are great to serve with dips or alongside your favourite curry.

INGREDIENTS:

120 g plain flour

½ tsp salt

½ tsp sugar

120 ml Greek yogurt

1 tbsp olive oil

Oil spray

1. Add the flour, salt and sugar to a large bowl and stir with a spoon to combine.
2. Add the yogurt and olive oil to the bowl with the flour. Stir the mixture with a spoon. You may need to use your hands to help bring the mixture together until it is all combined and there is no dry flour left in the bowl. If the mixture is too wet, add a bit more flour. If the mixture is too dry, add a bit more yogurt.
3. Divide the mixture into four evenly sized balls.
4. Sprinkle some flour onto your worktop and place one ball on top. Shape the ball into a flatbread by rolling it with a rolling pin into a circle roughly 12 cm wide. Repeat for the other three balls.
5. Preheat the air fryer to 200°C/400°F for 5 minutes.
6. Spray the top of each flatbread with a little oil. Carefully place the flatbreads into the air fryer basket, allowing a little space around each one. You may need to work in batches.
7. Set the temperature to 200°C/400°F and the timer for 4 minutes.
8. When the time is up, open the fryer and carefully turn the flatbreads over using tongs. Spray the top of each flatbread with a little oil before closing the fryer.
9. Set the temperature to 200 °C/400°F and the timer for 4 minutes.
10. When the time is up, open the fryer. The flatbreads should look brown and a little dry. If the flatbreads don't look as done as you would like, cook for another 1–2 minutes before checking again.
11. Carefully remove the flatbreads from the fryer using tongs.

CHEF IT UP! Instead of spraying the flatbreads with oil, try brushing them with a little garlic butter. Yum!

SUMMER

HOT HONEY CHICKEN STRIPS

SERVES 2 | TAKES 25 MINUTES

Take your air-fried chicken tender game to the next level with sticky hot honey sauce.

INGREDIENTS:

40 g plain flour

1 tsp salt

1 tsp ground black pepper

½ tsp onion powder

½ tsp garlic powder

1 tsp paprika

2 eggs, beaten

100 g dried breadcrumbs

500 g chicken strips or mini fillets

Oil spray

FOR THE HOT HONEY SAUCE:

120 ml honey

2 tbsp chilli flakes

1 tbsp lemon juice

CHEF IT UP!
These chicken strips would taste great in a wrap with some salad!

1. Add the flour into a medium bowl and add the salt, pepper, onion powder, garlic powder and paprika. Mix everything together with a spoon.
2. Crack the eggs into another medium bowl and whisk with a fork.
3. Pour the breadcrumbs onto a plate.
4. Take a mini fillet and toss it into the bowl with the flour and seasonings. Make sure the fillet is completely coated.
5. Dip the floured fillet in the egg. The flour will help the egg to stick to the chicken. Make sure it is well coated.
6. Place the egged fillet into the breadcrumbs. Turn the fillet in the breadcrumbs until it is completely covered.
7. Put the crumbed fillet on a clean plate.
8. Repeat steps 4–7 for the rest of your mini fillets. Add more breadcrumbs if you need to. Use your hands to help the breadcrumbs stick to the fillets.
9. Preheat the air fryer to 200°C/390°F for 5 minutes.

10 Spray each mini fillet with a little oil.

11 When the fryer is hot, place the mini fillets in the basket using tongs. Leave a bit of space around each fillet. You may need to work in batches. Set the temperature to 200°C/390°F and the timer for 5 minutes.

12 When the time is up, open the fryer and turn the mini fillets using a pair of tongs. Set the temperature to 200°C/390°F and the timer for 5 minutes.

13 Meanwhile, heat a small saucepan over a medium heat. Add the honey, chilli flakes and lemon juice, and stir. When the mixture starts to bubble, remove the saucepan from the heat and pour the contents into a medium bowl.

14 When the time is up, open the fryer. The mini fillets should look crisp and golden and there should be no pink meat inside. To check whether they are cooked, push a meat thermometer into the centre of one fillet. If the temperature reads 74°C/165°F or above, the chicken is cooked. If the temperature reads below 74°C/165°F or the chicken doesn't look as crisp as you would like, cook for another 2–3 minutes before checking again.

15 Carefully remove the chicken from the fryer using tongs and place in the bowl with the honey sauce. Toss the chicken in the sauce and serve while still hot.

PRAWN SCAMPI

SERVES 4 | TAKES 25 MINUTES

A batch of homemade scampi will bring you a taste of the seaside, wherever you eat them.

INGREDIENTS:

45 g plain flour

½ tsp paprika

½ tsp dried parsley

½ tsp garlic powder

½ tsp onion powder

½ tsp salt

½ tsp ground black pepper

2 eggs

80 g dried breadcrumbs

400 g large raw prawns, tails removed

Oil spray

1. Preheat the air fryer to 200°C/400°F for 5 minutes.
2. Add the flour, paprika, parsley, garlic powder, onion powder, salt and pepper into a medium bowl and mix together with a fork.
3. Crack the eggs into another medium bowl and beat with a fork.
4. Tip the breadcrumbs onto a plate.
5. Pat dry the prawns using kitchen roll.
6. Dip a prawn in the seasoned flour and shake off any excess.
7. Dip the floured prawn in the egg. Hold the prawn over the bowl for a few seconds to let any extra egg drip off.
8. Roll the eggy prawn in the breadcrumbs. Place the breaded prawn on a plate.
9. Repeat steps 6–8 for the rest of the prawns.
10. Spray the prawns with a little oil. Spray the air fryer basket with oil. Use tongs to carefully lay the prawns in the basket. Try to leave a few centimetres around each prawn. You may need to work in batches.
11. Set the temperature to 200°C/400°F and the timer for 5 minutes.
12. When the time is up, the prawns should look crisp and golden. Push a thermometer into the middle of a prawn. If fully cooked, the temperature should be 63°C/145°F or above. If the temperature is too low or the prawns do not look as done as you would like, close the fryer and cook for another 1–2 minutes before checking again.
13. Use tongs to carefully remove the prawns from the fryer.

GF

CRISPY 'CRAB' SNACKS

SERVES 2 | TAKES 25 MINUTES

These crunchy seaside snacks are packed with protein and so delicious you won't be able to keep your claws off them!

INGREDIENTS:

250 g seafood sticks

½ tbsp vegetable oil

½ tsp salt

½ tsp ground black pepper

1 tsp garlic powder

½ tsp ground ginger

½ tsp Chinese 5-spice powder

5 tbsp sweet chilli sauce to serve

1. Preheat the air fryer to 190°C/375°F for 5 minutes.
2. Unwrap the seafood sticks. Using a sharp knife and cutting board, cut each stick in half lengthways and then cut each strip in half lengthways again. It doesn't matter if the strips end up being different thicknesses, this makes for a more interesting snack!
3. Add the oil, salt, pepper and spices to medium bowl and stir with a spoon.
4. Mix the seafood strips with the oil and spices until they are well coated.
5. Tip the strips into the hot fryer basket and carefully spread them out evenly using tongs. It doesn't matter if some strips are on top of the other.
6. Set the temperature to 190°C/375°F and the timer for 7 minutes.
7. When the time is up, open the fryer. Give the basket a shake to loosen up the seafood strips. Use tongs to carefully turn the crispier pieces over.
8. Set the temperature to 190°C/375°F and the timer for 5 minutes.
9. When the time is up, open the fryer. The strips should look crisp and golden. If the strips don't look as crisp as you would like, return the basket to the fryer for 1 minute before checking again.
10. Carefully remove the strips from the basket using tongs and place them in bowl.
11. Serve fresh from the fryer, with a bowl of sweet chilli sauce. Any leftover sticks can be stored in an airtight container in the fridge and enjoyed cold.

CHEF IT UP!

Experiment by adding different flavours, such as a squeeze of lemon juice or paprika.

SUMMER

(VG) (GF)

HALLOUMI MINI SKEWERS

SERVES 2 | TAKES 20 MINUTES

These savoury cheese skewers are delicious served with a fresh salad and a warm flatbread (see page 29).

INGREDIENTS:

100 g halloumi

½ small onion

½ green pepper

8 cherry tomatoes

1 tbsp olive oil

1 tbsp lemon juice

½ tsp ground black pepper

1 tsp thyme

EQUIPMENT:

Metal skewers that fit in your air fryer or wooden skewers

Pastry brush

CHEF IT UP! Try brushing some different flavours on your halloumi. Sweet chilli sauce, soy sauce or honey would all taste delicious.

1. Cut the halloumi into cubes measuring about 2 cm and put to one side.
2. Cut the onion and the pepper into 2–3 cm chunks.
3. If using wooden skewers, remove the basket from the air fryer and check to see if they will fit in the basket. If the skewers are too long, cut or carefully break off enough of the blunt end of each skewer for them to fit without touching the sides.
4. Preheat the air fryer to 190°C/375°F for 5 minutes.
5. To assemble the skewers, push the sharp end of one skewer through the centre of a piece of halloumi. Then push a piece of onion, a piece of pepper and a tomato onto the skewer.
6. Repeat step 5 until the skewer is almost completely covered. Leave 2 cm of skewer bare at each end. This will help to stop pieces falling off when the skewers are removed from the fryer.
7. Repeat this until you have used up all the ingredients, or all of your skewers are filled.
8. Mix together the oil, lemon juice, black pepper and thyme in a small bowl.
9. Brush each skewer with the oil and lemon mixture.
10. Carefully place the skewers into the air fryer basket using tongs. Set the temperature to 190°C/375°F and the timer for 5 minutes.

11 When the time is up, open the fryer basket. The halloumi should have browned, and the vegetables should look crisp around the edges. If they don't look as cooked as you would like, close the fryer and cook for 2 minutes before checking again.

12 Remove the skewers from the fryer and brush with a little more of the oil and lemon before serving.

(VG)

AVOCADO DIPPERS

MAKES 8 DIPPERS | TAKES 25 MINUTES

A cooling avocado dip is delicious, but have you tried hot, crispy avocado dippers?

INGREDIENTS:

1 large avocado (ripe but not mushy)

4 tbsp plain flour

½ tsp salt

½ tsp garlic powder

½ tsp ground black pepper

½ tsp paprika

1 egg, beaten

70 g dried breadcrumbs

Oil spray

FOR THE DIP:

4 tbsp mayonnaise

1 tsp sriracha sauce

2 tsp fresh lime juice

CHEF IT UP!
Feeling cheesy? Add a tablespoon or two of grated parmesan cheese to the breadcrumbs for an even more savoury crunch.

1. Using a sharp knife, carefully slice into the avocado lengthways until you reach the pit. With the knife still inside, turn the avocado to slice the avocado in half around the pit. Remove the knife and twist the two halves apart. Use a spoon to scoop out the pit.
2. Cut each half of the avocado in half lengthways and then cut each of these halves in half lengthways again. This will give you eight slices of avocado.
3. Use a table knife or your thumb to remove the peel from each slice of avocado.
4. Add the flour, salt and spices to a plate or shallow dish and mix together with a fork.
5. Pour the beaten egg into a shallow dish. Tip the breadcrumbs onto a third plate.
6. Preheat the air fryer to 200°C/390°F for 5 minutes.
7. Take a piece of avocado and roll it in the flour until it is well coated.
8. Dip this piece of avocado into the egg. The egg will stick to the flour on the outside of the avocado.
9. Roll the eggy avocado in the breadcrumbs. Use your fingers to press the breadcrumbs onto the avocado. When the slice is well coated, put it on a plate.
10. Repeat steps 7–9 for each avocado slice and spray each one with a little oil.
11. Use tongs to carefully place the avocado slices into the fryer. Leave a little space around each slice.
12. Set the temperature to 200°C/390°F and the timer for 3 minutes.

13 While the dippers are cooking, add the mayonnaise, sriracha and fresh lime juice to a bowl and stir.

14 When the time is up, open the fryer and carefully turn the dippers using tongs. If the slices look dry, spray them with a little oil before closing the fryer. Set the temperature to 200°C/390°F and the timer for 3 minutes.

15 When the time is up, open the fryer. Your dippers should look crisp and golden. If they do not look as done as you would like, close the fryer and cook for another 1–2 minutes before checking again.

16 Carefully remove the dippers from the fryer using tongs. Serve straight away with the sauce on the side.

SUMMER

HAM AND CHEESE QUICHE

SERVES 4 | TAKES 25 MINUTES

This quick and easy quiche makes a perfect picnic dish or even a summer breakfast.

INGREDIENTS:

Oil spray

1 flour tortilla, roughly 25 cm wide

2 medium eggs

80 ml double cream

1 spring onion, chopped

2 slices ham, chopped

40 g cheddar cheese, grated

¼ tsp salt

¼ tsp ground black pepper

1 slice tomato, quartered

1 sprig basil (optional)

EQUIPMENT:

18-cm cake tin or a round tin that fits into your air fryer

CHEF IT UP! Fill your quiche with any vegetable and herb combinations you like. Feta and tomato, or broccoli and blue cheese work well.

1. Preheat the air fryer to 180°C/350°F for 5 minutes.
2. Spray the inside of the cake tin with oil. Press the tortilla into the bottom of the tin. It doesn't have to fit snugly. The tortilla edges should come 2–3 cm up the side of the tin.
3. In a jug, combine the eggs and the cream using a fork. Add the spring onion, ham, cheese, salt and pepper.
4. Pour the egg mixture into the tortilla-lined tin.
5. Place the tomato slices on top and the sprig of basil, if using.
6. Cover the tin with a piece of tin foil. Pinch the foil around the edge of the tin to make a seal.
7. Place the tin into the air fryer basket. Set the temperature to 180°C/350°F and the timer for 12 minutes.
8. When the time is up, remove the basket from the fryer. Use tongs to carefully remove the foil.
9. Return the basket to the fryer, set the temperature to 180°C/350°F and the timer for 10 minutes.

10 When the time is up, remove the basket from the fryer. Your quiche should look brown on top and crisp around the edges. If you are unsure whether it is cooked through, check the quiche using a thermometer. The temperature should read 70°C/160°F or higher. Or you can push a table knife in the middle: if it comes out clean the quiche is cooked. If it comes out with wet egg mixture on it, return the basket to the fryer and cook for another 2–3 minutes before checking again.

11 Carefully remove the quiche from the fryer using oven gloves. Leave it to cool a little in the tin on a wire rack.

12 Remove the quiche from the tin. If it feels soft or soggy on the bottom, put it back into the air fryer without the tin, and cook for another 1–2 minutes.

13 Serve warm or leave to cool completely and refrigerate to enjoy later.

SUMMER

VG

FALAFEL PITTA POCKETS

MAKES 4 | TAKES 25 MINUTES

These crunchy falafel patties are delicious served hot or cold. For a packed lunch or picnic treat, let the falafel cool completely before assembling your sandwich.

INGREDIENTS:

400 g tin chickpeas

¼ medium onion

2 cloves garlic

½ tsp ground cumin

½ tsp ground coriander

4 tbsp fresh coriander, chopped

4 tbsp fresh parsley, chopped

¼ tsp salt

¼ tsp ground black pepper

½ tsp baking powder

2 tbsp sesame seeds

4 pitta breads

4 lettuce leaves

FOR THE DRESSING:

6 tbsp Greek yogurt

1 x 6-cm-piece cucumber, grated

2 cloves garlic, crushed

1 tbsp fresh mint, chopped

2 tsp lemon juice

1 tbsp olive oil

¼ tsp salt

EQUIPMENT:

Food processor

CHEF IT UP!
Why not add a slice of tomato, gherkins or crumble on some feta cheese?

1. Drain the chickpeas using a colander or sieve. Rinse the chickpeas with water and then tip them out onto a few pieces of kitchen roll. Use another piece of kitchen roll to pat them dry.

2. Add the onion, garlic, cumin, coriander (ground and fresh), parsley, salt, pepper and baking powder to the bowl of a food processor. Add the chickpeas. Put the lid on the food processor and pulse the mixture until it looks like coarse wet sand.

3. Carefully remove the lid and the blade from the food processor. Divide the mixture into four. Use your hands to shape each portion into patties. Each patty should be about 2.5 centimetres thick. Sprinkle sesame seeds on top of each patty. Turn the patties over and sprinkle more seeds on the other side. Press the seeds in with your fingers so they stick to the patties.

4. Preheat the air fryer to 190°C/375°F for 5 minutes.

SUMMER

5 Place a paper liner into the air fryer basket. Place the patties on the liner. Set the temperature to 190°C/375°F and the timer for 8 minutes.

6 When the time is up, carefully turn the patties over using tongs. Put back in the fryer to cook for another 5 minutes.

7 While the falafel patties are cooking, make the dip. Add the yogurt, cucumber, garlic, oil, lemon juice and mint to a bowl and mix with a fork. Add the salt and stir again. Put to one side.

8 When the time is up, the falafel patties should look crisp and brown and be firm to the touch.

9 Remove the patties from the fryer using tongs. Remove the liner and throw it away.

10 Put the pitta breads into the air fryer. Set the temperature to 180°C/350°F and the timer for 2 minutes.

11 When the time is up, carefully remove the pittas from the fryer using tongs. Leave to cool for 1–2 minutes. Make a slit in the side of each pitta using a serrated knife. Open up the pitta at the slit using your fingers.

12 Spread 1 tbsp of dip inside each pitta. Place a piece of lettuce on top. Put a falafel patty on top of the lettuce and add more dip before closing the pitta. Serve with extra dip on the side.

LAMB SHISH KEBABS

MAKES 4–6 SKEWERS | TAKES 40 MINUTES PLUS 1–24 HOURS FOR MARINATING

A deliciously tender treat that tastes better than your local takeaway.

INGREDIENTS:

2 cloves garlic, grated or crushed

1 tbsp lemon juice

2 tbsp olive oil

½ tsp ground coriander

½ tsp cayenne pepper

½ tsp ground cumin

½ tsp ground black pepper

400 g lamb leg steak, cut into bite-sized pieces

½ red pepper

½ yellow pepper

½ green pepper

1 medium red onion

EQUIPMENT:

4–6 metal or wooden skewers

Pastry brush

CHEF IT UP! Add a couple of teaspoonfuls of mint sauce to some plain yogurt to make a delicious tangy dressing for your lamb.

1. Add the garlic, lemon juice, olive oil and spices to a large bowl and mix well with a fork.

2. Add the pieces of lamb to the bowl and toss them in the spiced oil. Make sure they are well coated. Cover the bowl and put it in the fridge for 1–24 hours. The longer you leave the lamb in the fridge, the more tender and flavoursome your kebabs will be.

3. If using wooden skewers, remove the air fryer basket and check to see if the skewers will fit inside. If they are too long, cut or carefully break off enough of the blunt end of each skewer for them to fit without touching the sides. Fill a bowl or tray with water and add the skewers. Leave them to soak until you are ready to cook. Soaking the skewers will stop them from burning in the air fryer.

4. When you are ready to cook, preheat the air fryer to 200°C/400°F for 5 minutes.

5. Use a sharp knife and a clean cutting board to carefully cut the stems off the peppers. Use a teaspoon to scrape out any seeds and white pith from inside the pepper. Cut the peppers into bite-sized pieces, similar to the size of the pieces of lamb. Put the pepper to one side.

6. Use the same knife and cutting board to cut the onion in half. Place the onion halves flat-side down and cut off the tip and root. Peel the papery skin from the onion. Cut each half of the onion into quarters. Don't worry if your onion quarters fall apart.

7. Remove the lamb from fridge. Take the skewers out of the water and pat them dry with a piece of kitchen roll.

8. To assemble the skewers, push the sharp end of one skewer through the centre of a piece of lamb. Then push a layer or two of onion and a piece of pepper onto the skewer. Repeat this until your skewer is almost full. Leave at least 2 cm of skewer bare at each end. This will help to stop pieces falling off when the skewers are removed from the fryer.

9. Repeat step 8 for each skewer.

10. Brush any remaining marinade in the bowl on the vegetables on each skewer.

11. Carefully place the skewers into the fryer basket using tongs. Set the temperature to 200°C/400°F and the timer for 5 minutes.

12. When the time is up, open the fryer. Use tongs to carefully turn each skewer. If you have any remaining marinade in the bowl, brush it onto any dry-looking areas of your kebabs. Set the temperature to 200°C/400°F and the timer for 5 minutes.

13. When the time is up, open the fryer. The lamb should have browned, and the vegetables should have crisped and blackened at the edges. To be sure that the skewers are cooked, insert a thermometer into the centre of a piece of lamb. If the thermometer reads 63°C/145°F, the lamb is cooked. Don't worry if your lamb pieces are a little bit pink inside. If the temperature is lower than this, or the kebabs don't look as well done as you would like, cook them at 200°C/400°F for another 3–5 minutes before checking again.

14. Carefully remove the kebabs from the fryer using tongs.

15. Serve hot with flatbreads (see page 29) and a crunchy, fresh salad.

VG VE GF

ROASTED CAULIFLOWER STEAKS

MAKES 2 STEAKS | TAKES 30 MINUTES

These veggie steaks are a juicy and delicious alternative to the meat variety.

INGREDIENTS:

1 medium cauliflower, whole

3 tbsp olive oil

1 tsp garlic powder

1 tsp onion powder

1 tsp smoked paprika

½ tsp salt

½ tsp ground black pepper

EQUIPMENT:

Pastry brush

FOR THE SAUCE:

5 tbsp olive oil

1 tbsp white wine vinegar

30 g fresh parsley, chopped

1 clove garlic, crushed

½ tsp salt

½ tsp chilli flakes

¼ tsp dried oregano

CHEF IT UP! Don't have a cauliflower? No problem. Substitute the cauliflower with a cabbage. Cut it into steaks in the same way as the cauliflower. Delicious!

1. Add the oil, garlic powder, onion powder, spoked paprika, salt and pepper to a small bowl and mix with a fork.

2. Preheat the air fryer to 200°C/400°F for 5 minutes.

3. Peel off any leaves from the outside of the cauliflower and throw them away. Put the cauliflower onto a cutting board stalk-side down. Hold the cauliflower firmly with one hand. Use a sharp knife to cut the cauliflower into slices about 3 cm thick. One cauliflower should make 2 proper 'steaks' and lots of florets that you can marinate and cook in the same way. They'll still taste delicious!

4. Arrange the slices on a plate. Use a pastry brush to brush the cauliflower steaks with the oil mixture. Turn the steaks over and brush the other side.

5. Use tongs to arrange the steaks in the air fryer basket. Try to leave a little space around each one. You may need to work in batches. Set the temperature to 200°C/400°F and the timer for 6 minutes.

6   When the time is up, carefully turn the steaks over using tongs and brush on some of the remaining oil mixture. Set the temperature to 200°C/400°F and the timer for 6 minutes.

7   To make the sauce, add the olive oil, vinegar, garlic, chilli flakes and oregano to a bowl and mix using a fork. Add the chopped parsley and stir. Put this to one side.

8   When the time is up, the steaks should look golden brown and crispy around the edges. To check if they are cooked, push a fork into the centre of one steak. The fork should slide in easily. If the steak still feels a little tough, cook for another 2–3 minutes before checking again.

9   Remove the steaks from the fryer using tongs. Serve hot with a spoonful or two of the sauce.

SUMMER

CARAMELIZED PINEAPPLE

SERVES 2 | TAKES 20 MINUTES

This hot, tropical treat makes a tasty alternative to fruit salad. Serve with ice cream or yogurt.

INGREDIENTS:

- ½ fresh pineapple
- 25 g brown sugar
- 30 g butter, melted
- ½ tsp ground cinnamon
- ¼ tsp ground nutmeg
- 2 scoops vanilla ice cream

EQUIPMENT:

Pastry brush

1. Use a serrated knife and a cutting board to carefully slice the top and bottom off the pineapple. Stand the pineapple up on one of its cut sides and cut it in half from top to bottom. You will only use half the pineapple for this recipe. Store the other half in the fridge to enjoy later.

2. Place the pineapple half cut-side down on the cutting board and cut it in half lengthways. Place each quarter cut-side down on the cutting board and cut away the core. This is the hard middle bit of the pineapple. It won't do you any harm if you eat it, but it can be a bit tough.

3. Put the cored pieces, skin-side down and cut them in half lengthways again to make pineapple sticks. Then carefully cut away the skin.

4. Preheat the air fryer to 200°C/400°F for 5 minutes.

5. Add the sugar, cinnamon and nutmeg to a medium bowl. Add the melted butter and stir until all mixed together.

6. Toss the pineapple in the spiced sugar and butter until it is well coated.

7. Use tongs to carefully arrange the pineapple in the air fryer basket. Set the temperature to 200°C/400°F and the timer for 5 minutes.

8. When the time is up, open the fryer and use tongs to carefully turn each piece of pineapple. If they are looking a little dry, brush them with any remaining butter and sugar mix. Set the temperature to 200°C/400°F and the timer for 5 minutes.

9. When the time is up, open the fryer. The pineapple should have darkened in colour and be crisp around the edges.

10. Carefully remove the pineapple from the fryer using tongs.

11. Serve with a scoop of ice cream.

GF

CHOCOLATE MARSHMALLOW FONDUE WITH MINI FRUIT SKEWERS

MAKES 1 FONDUE | TAKES 10 MINUTES

This gooey pot of yumminess is ready in minutes. Serve with your favourite fruit for an extra-special summer snack.

INGREDIENTS:

60 g dark chocolate chips

4–6 large marshmallows

4 strawberries

1 banana, sliced

6 pineapple chunks

1 handful blackberries

EQUIPMENT:

Ramekin, roughly 9 cm x 5 cm or 200 ml capacity

CHEF IT UP!
Use whatever fruit is your favourite. Everything tastes good with melted chocolate!

1. Preheat the air fryer to 190°C/375°F for 5 minutes.
2. Put the chocolate chips in the bottom of the ramekin.
3. Arrange the marshmallows on top of the chocolate chips.
4. Use tongs or oven gloves to carefully place the ramekin into the air fryer basket. Set the temperature to 190°C/375°F and the timer for 5 minutes.
5. When the time is up, open the fryer. The marshmallows should look golden and puffy. If they do not look as cooked as you would like, close the fryer and cook for another minute before checking again.
6. Use tongs or oven gloves to carefully remove the ramekin from the fryer and put it on a plate.
7. Serve immediately alongside the fruit.

VG

STRAWBERRIES AND CREAM BUTTERFLY CAKES

MAKES 6–8 CUPCAKES | TAKES 45 MINUTES

While fresh summer strawberries and cream are delicious all by themselves, this cupcake recipe transforms them into a perfect party treat.

INGREDIENTS:

1 egg, large

70 g caster sugar

110 g plain flour

¾ tsp baking powder

75 ml milk

50 g butter

½ tsp vanilla extract

3 strawberries, chopped

FOR THE TOPPING:

110 ml double cream

20 g icing sugar

¼ tsp vanilla extract

2–3 strawberries, quartered

EQUIPMENT:

Microwave

Electric whisk

6–8 silicone cupcake cases

CHEF IT UP! Swap out the strawberries for any fruit you like. Peaches and cream, anyone?

1. Crack the egg into a medium bowl and add the sugar, flour and baking powder.
2. Whisk together the ingredients until the mixture looks like sand and then put to one side.
3. Add the milk and the butter to a microwave-safe bowl or measuring jug.
4. Microwave the butter and milk for 30 seconds. After 30 seconds, check to see whether the butter has melted. If it is still solid, return it to the microwave for another 30 seconds. Repeat until the butter has just melted.

5. Pour the milk and butter into the flour mixture. Add the vanilla extract and mix until there are no big lumps (little sandy lumps are okay). Add the chopped strawberries and mix gently.

6. Spoon the mixture into the silicone cupcake cases, filling each until it is about three-quarters full.

7. Preheat the air fryer to 180°C/325°F for 5 minutes.

8. Use tongs to carefully place the cupcakes in the air fryer basket. Set the temperature to 180°C/325°F and the timer for 15 minutes.

9. When the time is up, check your cupcakes. They should be risen and golden. To make extra sure they are cooked, insert a table knife into the centre of one cupcake and pull it out. If the knife is clean when you pull it out, the cupcakes are ready! If the knife has raw cake mix on it, put the cupcakes back in the fryer for 2–3 more minutes and then check again.

10. Use tongs to carefully remove your cupcakes from the fryer basket and place them on a cooling rack.

11. To make the topping, pour the double cream, icing sugar and vanilla extract into a large mixing bowl. Use an electric whisk set to a low speed to whip the mixture until the cream thickens. Whip the cream until it is thick enough to hold its shape when you remove the whisk.

12. Use a sharp knife to cut the strawberries into quarters, lengthways.

13. Slice the top off each cupcake, then cut each top piece in half.

14. Spoon a good dollop of cream onto the top of each cupcake.

15. Arrange the halved cupcake tops on the cream, sticking up slightly.

16. Place a strawberry quarter into the centre of each cupcake.

17. Dust with a little extra icing sugar and serve immediately.

SUMMER

JAMMY FRENCH TOAST ROLL-UPS

MAKES 4 ROLL-UPS | TAKES 20 MINUTES

These jammy French toast rolls are crispy, sweet, creamy and impossible to resist.

INGREDIENTS:

- 60 g cream cheese
- 2 tsp icing sugar
- ½ tsp vanilla extract
- 1 egg, beaten
- 4 tsp granulated sugar
- 4 tbsp milk
- 4 slices white bread
- 4 tsp jam
- Oil spray

1. Preheat the air fryer to 160°C/325°F for 5 minutes.
2. Add the cream cheese, icing sugar and vanilla extract to a small bowl and mix together using a spoon. Put to one side.
3. Add the egg, 1 tsp of the granulated sugar, and the milk to a medium bowl and beat together using a fork. Put to one side.
4. Take a slice of bread and cut off the crusts using a table knife.
5. Put the slice of bread onto a clean work surface and use a rolling pin to roll it flat until it no longer springs back.
6. Repeat steps 4–5 with the rest of the bread.
7. Spread each slice of bread with one-quarter of the cream cheese mixture using a table knife.
8. Spread 1 tbsp of jam on top of the cream cheese mixture.
9. Roll up each slice of bread into a sausage shape. Press each roll into the mixture to help to keep it closed. If the rolls look like they are about to spring open, secure them by pushing a cocktail stick through each end.
10. Dip each roll into the egg mixture and make sure they are well covered. Put the rolls on a plate.
11. Spray the rolls with a little oil. Use tongs to carefully place the rolls into the air fryer basket. Set the temperature to 160°C/325°F and the timer for 8 minutes.
12. Add the rest of the sugar to a plate.
13. When the time is up, open the fryer. The rolls should look crisp and golden and a little brown around the edges. If the rolls don't look as done as you would like, close the fryer and cook for another 1–2 minutes before checking again.
14. Remove the rolls from the fryer using tongs and put them on the plate with the sugar. If you used cocktail sticks, remove these now. Roll the hot rolls in the sugar. Leave to cool for a few minutes before enjoying. Be careful, the jam inside will be hot!

SUMMER

AIR-FRIED ALASKA

MAKES 4 ALASKAS | TAKES 30 MINUTES PLUS 1 HOUR FREEZING TIME

What's piping hot and crispy on the outside but freezing cold on the inside and is sure to become a new favourite dessert? Air-fried Alaska!

INGREDIENTS:

4 digestive biscuits

4 large scoops of vanilla ice cream

2 egg whites

30 g caster sugar

EQUIPMENT:

Electric whisk

1. Place four digestive biscuits on a piece of greaseproof paper on top of a plate or small tray.

2. Scoop a ball of ice cream and place one on top of each biscuit. Put the plate into the freezer for 1 hour.

3. Add the egg whites and sugar to a large bowl. Whisk using an electric whisk. The mixture will turn white and fluffy. Continue to whisk until the mixture is thick enough to keep its shape when you take out the whisk.

4. Remove the ice cream from the freezer. Take one ice cream biscuit from the plate.

5. Tip the ice cream biscuit upside down and dip it into the meringue. Use a spoon to help coat the ice cream in the egg white mixture. When it is completely covered, put it back onto the plate. Repeat for the other three ice cream biscuits.

6. Place the plate with the Alaskas on back in the freezer.

7. Preheat the air fryer to 200°C/400°F for 5 minutes.

8. Remove the plate from the freezer. Use a spatula to remove one Alaska from the plate and put it into the air fryer basket on top of a paper liner. Set the temperature to 200°C/400°F and the timer for 4 minutes. Return the plate with the rest of the Alaskas to the freezer. These are best when cooked one at a time.

9. When the time is up, open the fryer. The meringue should look brown and be firm to the touch. Don't worry if the ice cream is leaking a little bit, it will still taste delicious.

10. Use a spatula to carefully remove the baked ice cream from the fryer.

11. Serve this one before starting on the next.

CHEF IT UP!

Experiment with different toppings. Sliced banana with chocolate sauce and nuts is delicious on top of your baked Alaska.

AUTUMN

VG VE GF

PUMPKIN SOUP

SERVES 4 | TAKES 40–55 MINUTES

There's nothing better than a rich and creamy bowl of pumpkin soup to warm yourself up on an autumn day.

INGREDIENTS:

2 tbsp olive oil

½ tsp salt

½ tsp ground black pepper

½ tsp ground cumin

½ tsp ground cinnamon

½ tsp paprika

700 g pumpkin, cut into 3-cm cubes

1 medium onion, peeled and quartered

2 cloves garlic, peeled

2 medium tomatoes, quartered

1 red pepper, deseeded and cut into 3-cm pieces

250 ml vegetable stock

80 ml coconut milk

EQUIPMENT:

Hand blender, liquidizer or food processor

CHEF IT UP!

If pumpkins aren't available in the shops, butternut squash is an excellent substitute here.

1. Preheat the air fryer to 180°C/360°F for 5 minutes.
2. Pour the olive oil into a large bowl. Add the salt, pepper and spices and stir well with a fork.
3. Add the pumpkin, onion, garlic, tomatoes and red pepper to the bowl. Toss the vegetables until all the chunks are coated with the spiced oil.
4. Place a liner in the bottom of the fryer basket. Use tongs to carefully arrange the vegetables on the liner. Try to leave a little space around each piece to allow them to cook evenly. You may need to do this step in batches.
5. Set the temperature to 180°C/360°F and the timer for 20 minutes.
6. When the time is up, open the fryer. Your vegetables should look a little browned around the edges. Press a fork into a piece of the pumpkin. The prongs should slide easily into the pumpkin. If the pumpkin is still hard or the vegetables are not as brown as you would like, cook for another 5 minutes before checking again.
7. When the vegetables are ready, carefully tip them into a large pan. Add the vegetable stock.

8. Put the pan on the hob. Heat the pan over a medium to high heat until it begins to bubble. Stir the vegetables in the pan using a wooden spoon. When the pan begins to boil, turn the heat down to low. Add the coconut milk and stir.

9. Cook the vegetables in the stock and coconut milk for 10 minutes.

10. Carefully remove the pan from the hob and put it on a heatproof mat.

11. Ask an adult to help you with the next step. Use a hand blender to transform all of the chunky vegetables into a smooth and silky soup. If you do not have a hand blender, tip the vegetables and stock into a liquidizer or food processor.

12. Ladle the soup into four bowls and serve with a slice of soda bread (see page 12).

AUTUMN

CHICKEN TIKKA BITES

SERVES 2-4 | TAKES 30 MINUTES PLUS 1 HOUR CHILLING TIME

These chicken tikka bites are tender and delicious. Serve with a crunchy salad and flatbread (see page 29).

INGREDIENTS:

500 g chicken breast

200 g plain yogurt

1 tbsp grated ginger

2 cloves garlic, crushed

1 tsp salt

1 tsp ground turmeric

1 tsp ground coriander

1 tsp ground cumin

1 tsp garam masala

Oil spray

EQUIPMENT:

Wooden or metal skewers

Meat thermometer

CHEF IT UP!

Mix any leftover chicken tikka bites with a little mayonnaise and chopped coriander or leftover yogurt dip to make a delicious chicken tikka sandwich.

1. Use a sharp knife and a cutting board to cut the chicken into 3-cm chunks.
2. Put the yogurt, ginger, garlic, salt and spices into a large bowl and stir.
3. Add the chicken to the bowl and stir. Make sure all of the chicken is coated in the yogurt and spices.
4. Cover the bowl and put it in the fridge for 1 hour.
5. If using wooden skewers, remove the air fryer basket and check to see if they will fit. If the skewers are too long, cut or carefully break off enough of the blunt end of each skewer for them to fit without touching the sides. Fill a large bowl or tray with water and add the skewers. Leave them to soak until it is time to remove the chicken from the fridge. Soaking the skewers will stop them from burning in the air fryer.
6. Preheat the air fryer to 180°C/350°F for 5 minutes.
7. Remove the chicken from fridge. Take the skewers out of the water and pat them dry with a piece of paper towel.
8. To assemble the skewers, push the sharp end of one skewer through the centre of a piece of chicken.
9. Repeat with another piece of chicken until the skewer is almost completely covered. Leave 2 cm of skewer bare at each end. This will help to stop pieces falling off when the skewers are removed from the fryer.

10 Repeat this until you have used all your ingredients, or all of your skewers are filled.

11 Spray the air fryer basket with a little oil. Arrange the skewers in the basket, leaving a bit of space around each one. Don't crowd the skewers together. You may need to work in batches.

12 Set the temperature to 180°C/350°F and the timer for 6 minutes.

13 When the time is up, use tongs to carefully turn the skewers over. Set the temperature to 180°C/350°F and the timer for 6 minutes.

14 When the time is up, open the fryer basket. The chicken should look crisp around the edges and there should be no pink meat inside. To check whether it is cooked, push the tip of a thermometer into the centre of one piece of chicken. If the temperature reads 74°C/165°F or above, the chicken is cooked. If the chicken isn't quite ready, cook for another 2–3 minutes before checking again.

15 Carefully remove the skewers from the fryer using tongs and put them on a clean plate. Use a fork to push the meat off the skewers.

16 Serve hot with a flatbread (see page 29) or rice and salad.

MASALA-SPICED MIXED NUTS

SERVES 2 | TAKES 15 MINUTES

These spiced nuts are at their most delicious served warm, but make a wonderful gift when put into a nice jar.

INGREDIENTS:

30 g gram (chickpea) flour

20 g rice flour

1 tbsp brown sugar

1 tsp ground turmeric

½ tsp chilli powder

1 tsp garam masala

½ tsp salt

2 tbsp lime juice

1 tbsp oil

200 g nuts (raw shelled peanuts, walnuts, cashew nuts or pistachios all work well)

1. Preheat the air fryer to 175°C/350°F for 5 minutes.

2. Add the gram flour, rice flour, brown sugar, turmeric, chilli powder, garam masala and salt to a bowl. Mix together and put to one side.

3. Add the oil and lime juice to a separate bowl and stir well. Add the nuts and toss in the oil and lime-juice mixture. Add the dry ingredients to the bowl and mix together until the nuts are well coated in the spiced flour. If there is still a lot of loose flour in the bowl, add 1–2 tbsp of water and mix again.

4. Spray the air fryer basket with a little oil. Add the nuts. Try to leave a little space around the clumps of nuts. You may need to work in batches.

5. Set the temperature to 175°C/350°F and the timer for 5 minutes.

6. When the time is up, open the fryer. Give the basket a shake to turn some of the nuts over. Break up any large clumps using tongs. Spray the nuts with a little more oil.

7. Set the temperature of the fryer to 175°C/350°F and the timer for 2 minutes.

8. When the time is up, open the fryer. The nuts should look browned and the spiced coating look nice and crispy. If they don't look as done as you would like, close the fryer and cook for another 1–2 minutes before checking again.

9. Carefully tip the spiced nuts onto a piece of kitchen roll. Leave them to cool for a few minutes and serve.

Warning! This recipe contains nuts. Make sure none of your family or friends have nut allergies before sharing this dish with them.

CHEESE MUMMIES

MAKES 6 | TAKES 25 MINUTES

Turn a popular cheese snack into a terrifyingly tasty treat!

INGREDIENTS:

1 tbsp flour

320 g pack puff pastry sheet, room temperature

6 mini round snacking cheeses

6 tsp cranberry sauce or apricot jam

12 sliced black olives

1. Sprinkle the flour onto a clean work surface. Unroll the pastry and lay it on top of the flour. Use a ruler and a table knife to cut six, equally sized squares measuring approximately 10 x 10 cm and put them to one side.

2. Use a table knife to cut the rest of the pastry into strips measuring approximately 0.5 cm in width. These can be pretty rough as they will be your bandages.

3. Place 1 tsp of cranberry sauce or apricot jam in the centre of each square.

4. Unwrap the cheeses and place one cheese in the middle of each pastry square. Fold the corners of the square over the top of the cheese. Pinch the edges together to seal.

5. Preheat the air fryer to 180°C/350°F for 5 minutes.

6. Turn the pastry-wrapped cheese over so that the sealed side is underneath. Place two olive slices on top of each parcel to make eyes.

7. Use your fingers or a pastry brush to apply a little water to the strips of pastry.

8. Arrange the pastry strips water-side down on top of the cheese parcels. Try to let the olive slices peek out from behind the strips. Tuck the ends of the strips underneath the parcel.

9. Use tongs to carefully put the pastry parcels into the air fryer basket. Set the temperature to 180°C/350°F and the timer for 12 minutes.

10. When the time is up, the pastry parcels should look crisp and golden. Carefully remove one parcel from the fryer using tongs. Turn it upside down onto a plate to check that it is crispy on both sides.

11. If your parcel does not look as done as you would like, return it to the air fryer basket and cook for another 2–3 minutes before checking again.

12. Carefully remove the parcels from the fryer using tongs, then leave to cool for a few minutes before serving. Warning, they're hot inside!

GARLIC-STUFFED MUSHROOMS

SERVES 2 | TAKES 40 MINUTES

These garlicky, mushroomy bites make a sensational starter or side dish.

INGREDIENTS:

10 medium mushrooms

1 tbsp olive oil

½ medium onion, chopped

3 cloves garlic, crushed or grated

½ tsp dried thyme

¼ tsp salt

¼ tsp ground black pepper

30 g cheddar cheese, grated

2 tbsp dried breadcrumbs

Oil spray

CHEF IT UP! For a more meaty snack, why not try adding some crumbled crispy bacon to the stuffing?

1. To prepare the mushrooms, use a clean, damp cloth or kitchen roll to wipe any dirt from the caps. Pull out the mushrooms' stalks. If the stalks look nice and fresh, use a sharp knife and a chopping board to cut them up into small pieces and put them to one side.

2. Add the oil to a small frying pan and heat it over a medium heat. Add the onions and the chopped mushroom stalks to the pan and stir.

3. Heat the onions and mushroom stalks for 3–5 minutes until the onions start to soften and the mushroom stalks darken a little. Keep an eye on them and stir now and then. Turn the heat down if the mixture looks like it is starting to burn.

4. Stir in the garlic, thyme, salt and pepper and cook for another 2 minutes before turning off the heat.

5. Spoon the onion and garlic mixture into a large bowl. Leave to cool for 5 minutes.

6. Preheat the air fryer to 190°C/325°F for 5 minutes.

7. When the onion mixture is cool enough to touch, add the grated cheese and stir.

8. Spray each mushroom cap with a little oil and add a heaped teaspoon of mixture into each one. Divide any extra mixture evenly between each mushroom.

9 Sprinkle the breadcrumbs on top of each mushroom and spray with a little oil.

10 Use tongs to put the stuffed mushrooms into the air fryer basket. Try to leave a little space around each of them. You may need to work in batches.

11 Set the temperature to 190°C/325°F and the timer for 15 minutes.

12 When the time is up, open the fryer. The breadcrumbs should look crisp and golden, and the cheese should have melted. To check if they are cooked, press the blade of a table knife into the centre of one mushroom. The mushroom should feel softer and spongier than when it was raw. If the mushroom feels firm, or does not look as done as you would like, cook for another 2–3 minutes before checking again.

13 Remove the mushrooms from the fryer using tongs, and serve while still hot.

VG VE

PUMPKIN-SPICED GRANOLA

MAKES 4–6 SERVINGS | TAKES 1 HOUR 20 MINUTES

This crunchy spiced granola is packed with all of your favourite autumn flavours.

INGREDIENTS:

FOR THE PUMPKIN MIX:

½ tsp ground cinnamon

½ tsp ground ginger

½ tsp allspice

1 pinch ground (or a few gratings of whole) nutmeg

1 pinch ground cloves

FOR THE GRANOLA:

2 tbsp vegetable oil

5 tbsp honey

½ tsp salt

250 g rolled oats

50 g tbsp pumpkin seeds

50 g pecans

50 g sliced almonds

50 g walnuts, chopped

50 g dried cranberries or raisins

1. Preheat the air fryer to 140°C/280°F for 5 minutes.
2. Add the cinnamon, ginger, allspice, nutmeg and cloves to a small bowl. Mix together with a spoon and put to one side.
3. Add the oil, honey and salt to a large bowl. Use a fork or whisk to mix them together.
4. Add the pumpkin spice to the bowl and mix well.
5. Add the oats, pumpkin seeds, pecans, almonds, chopped walnuts and dried fruit, and stir until all the dry ingredients are coated in the spiced oil and honey.
6. Place a liner in the basket of your air fryer. Spread a 2–3 cm layer of the granola mixture on top of the liner. You may need to work in batches.
7. Set the temperature to 140°C/280°F and the timer for 25 minutes.
8. When the time is up, open the fryer. The granola should look crisp and golden, if it looks a little pale, return the basket to the fryer, and cook for another 4–5 minutes.

9 When the granola is done, remove the basket from the fryer.

10 Leave the granola to cool in the basket for 10–15 minutes.

11 Take the liner out of the basket and place straight onto a plate.

12 Put the plate in the fridge to chill for 30 minutes.

13 When the granola is chilled, break up the granola into bite-sized chunks.

14 Serve your granola with cold milk or yogurt. The granola can be stored in an airtight jar or container in the fridge for up to a week.

Warning! This recipe contains nuts. Make sure none of your family or friends have nut allergies before sharing this granola with them.

CHEF IT UP!
Try adding any nuts and dried fruit that you like. Or stir some into your favourite muffin recipe before baking. Yum!

VG

SPRING GREEN MATCHA BISCUITS

MAKES 7–10 BISCUITS | TAKES 45 MINUTES

Eating your greens is much easier if they come in biscuit form!

INGREDIENTS:

110 g butter, melted

160 g brown sugar

¼ tsp salt

1 tsp vanilla extract

170 g plain flour

1 tbsp matcha powder

¼ tsp baking powder

1 medium egg, room temperature

60 g white chocolate chips

1. Add the melted butter, sugar, salt and vanilla to a large bowl and mix with a wooden spoon. Don't worry if the butter and sugar don't mix completely, this will be fixed in the next step.
2. Add the flour, matcha powder, baking powder and the egg and mix until you have a thick, sticky dough. Gently stir in the chocolate chips.
3. Use your hands to shape the dough into a cylinder shape, about 15–20 cm long. Wrap the cylinder in cling film and put in the fridge to chill for 30 minutes.
4. Remove the cylinder from fridge and unwrap it.
5. Use a sharp knife to cut the cylinder into 2-cm slices.
6. Arrange the slices about 3 cm apart on a liner. You may need to bake the biscuits in batches.
7. Preheat the air fryer to 150°C/300°F for 5 minutes.
8. Carefully place the liner into the air fryer basket. Set the temperature to 150°C/300°F and the timer for 8 minutes.
9. When the time is up, open the fryer and check your biscuits. They should look a little dry on top. If they look done, carefully take the liner out of the fryer and place onto a cooling rack. If the biscuits still look a bit wet, put them back into the air fryer for 2 minutes, and then check again.
10. Leave to cool for 5 minutes before eating.

CHEF IT UP!

These biscuits are great for a spooky Halloween party! Mould into a finger shape and use a white chocolate chip or walnut or almond half as a fingernail.

AUTUMN

PARKIN MINI LOAF

MAKES 1 MINI LOAF | TAKES 35 MINUTES

This ginger loaf is small enough to fit in the smallest fryers.

INGREDIENTS:

50 g butter, plus a little extra for greasing

60 g golden syrup

40 g brown sugar

25 g rolled oats

60 g plain flour

½ tsp bicarbonate of soda

1 tsp ground ginger

½ tsp ground cinnamon

½ tsp ground nutmeg

1 egg, beaten

EQUIPMENT:

Mini loaf tins, roughly 14.5 cm by 8.5 cm

1. Prepare a mini loaf tin by greasing the inside with butter using a piece of kitchen roll. Make sure the tin is completely covered.
2. Add the butter, golden syrup and brown sugar to a small saucepan and heat over a medium heat. Stir the mixture until the butter has melted and all of the sugar has dissolved. It does not need to boil.
3. Preheat the air fryer to 160°C/320°F for 5 minutes.
4. Add the oats, flour, bicarbonate of soda, ginger, cinnamon and nutmeg to a large bowl and mix together well. Pour in the melted butter and sugar mixture and stir.
5. Add the beaten egg to the bowl and stir.
6. Pour the batter into the greased loaf tin.
7. Carefully place the tin into the air fryer basket. Set the temperature to 160°C/320°F and the timer for 25 minutes.
8. When the time is up, open the fryer. The top of the parkin should have browned and the centre should look set and not wobbly. To check if it is cooked, push a knife into the middle of the loaf. The blade should come out clean with just a few crumbs. If the blade has uncooked batter on it, close the fryer and cook for another 3–5 minutes before checking again.
9. Carefully remove the parkin from the fryer using oven gloves and place it on a cooling rack.

AUTUMN

SPICED APPLE CAKE

SERVES 6-8 | TAKES 1 HOUR

Autumn means apples aplenty! Make this autumnal apple cake for a delicious after school treat.

INGREDIENTS:

Oil spray

180 g plain flour

½ tsp baking powder

½ tsp bicarbonate of soda

½ tsp ground cinnamon

½ tsp ground nutmeg

½ tsp salt

100 g light brown sugar

120 ml olive oil

1 medium egg

1 medium apple, cored and chopped into 1-cm chunks, plus a few thin slices to decorate

1 tbsp icing sugar, for dusting

EQUIPMENT:

18-cm cake tin or a round tin that fits into your air fryer

1. Spray the inside of the cake tin with oil so that it is well coated.
2. Add the flour, baking powder, bicarbonate of soda, cinnamon, nutmeg and salt to a large bowl and mix well.
3. In another bowl, whisk together the sugar, olive oil and egg. Make sure they are whisked together until they no longer separate and have increased in volume a little.
4. Preheat the air fryer to 160°C/325°F for 5 minutes.
5. Pour the liquid mixture into the dry mixture and mix together well. The batter will be very thick. Don't worry, this is fine.
6. Add the chopped apples and stir to combine.
7. Scrape the batter into the oiled cake tin. Press it into the edges using the back of a spoon and smooth out the top.
8. Lay a few thin slices of apple on top of the batter for decoration.
9. Cover the tin with a piece of tin foil. Crimp around the edges to seal the foil to the tin.
10. Carefully place the apple cake into the air fryer basket. Set the temperature to 160°C/325°F and the timer for 20 minutes.
11. When the time is up, open the air fryer. Carefully remove the foil from the top of the cake tin using tongs.
12. Set the temperature to 160°C/325°F and the timer for 18 minutes.

AUTUMN

13 When the time is up, carefully remove the cake tin from the fryer using tongs or oven gloves and set it down on a heatproof mat. The cake should look golden brown and crisp on top. To check if it is cooked through, push a table knife into the centre of the cake. The blade should come out clean with just a few crumbs. If the blade is covered in batter or the top doesn't look as cooked as you would like, return the cake tin to the fryer and cook for another 5 minutes before checking again.

14 Carefully remove the cake from the fryer using oven gloves and place on a cooling rack.

15 When the cake tin is cool enough to handle, run a table knife around the inside of the tin to help loosen the cake from the sides.

16 Place a plate upside down on top of the tin. Hold the plate and tin together, and then turn them over. Lift up the cake tin. The cake should slide out easily onto the plate. If it doesn't, repeat step 15 before turning it over with the plate and giving it a little shake. Turn the cake right-side up.

17 To decorate your cake, put the icing sugar into a sieve and hold the sieve over the cake. Tap the sides of the sieve with your hand to dust the cake with icing sugar.

VG

CHOCOLATE CHIP CATHERINE WHEELS

MAKES 16 PASTRIES | TAKES 25 MINUTES PLUS 30–60 MINUTES CHILLING TIME

These chocolate pastry swirls make a delicious and filling breakfast!

INGREDIENTS:

200 g cream cheese

2 tbsp sugar

1 egg, beaten

A little flour for dusting

320 g puff pastry

75 g chocolate chips

30 g pistachio nuts, chopped

1 tbsp honey

EQUIPMENT:

Pastry brush

1. Add the cream cheese, sugar and 1 tbsp of the beaten egg to a medium bowl and mix together using a spoon or whisk. Mix until all the ingredients are thoroughly blended.

2. Sprinkle a little flour onto a clean work surface. If your pastry comes as a sheet, unroll it and lay it on top of the flour. If the pastry comes in a block, place the pastry onto your floured work surface and use a rolling pin to roll it into a rectangle measuring around 35 x 25 cm. Turn the sheet so that the long edge is closest to you.

3. Spoon the cream cheese mixture onto the pastry. Spread it out using a table knife leaving 2 cm of the pastry uncovered at the long edge furthest from you. Sprinkle the chocolate chips and three-quarters of the nuts over the cheese.

4. Fold the long edge of the pastry closest to you onto the filling and then continue to roll until you have a long sausage shape. Brush the unfilled edge of pastry with a little water and fold it over the top to seal the roll. Wrap the roll in cling film and place it in the fridge to chill for 30–60 minutes.

5. Preheat the air fryer to 160°C/325°F for 5 minutes.

6. Remove the roll from the fridge and unwrap it. Use a sharp knife to cut the roll into slices, around 1.5 cm thick. Brush each slice with the remaining beaten egg.

7. Use tongs to carefully place the rolls in the air fryer basket. Try to leave a little space around each roll. You may need to work in batches.

8. Set the temperature to 160°C/325°F and the timer for 15 minutes.

9. When the time is up, open the fryer. The pastries should have puffed up and look crisp and golden brown. If the pastries don't look as done as you would like, cook for another 1–2 minutes before checking again.

10. Remove the pastries from the fryer using tongs and put them on a plate.

11. To serve, drizzle the pastries with a little honey and sprinkle over the remaining nuts.

Warning! This recipe contains nuts. Make sure none of your family or friends have nut allergies before sharing these pastries with them.

AUTUMN

VG

FIRECRACKER BISCUITS

MAKES 16–18 BISCUITS | TAKES 20 MINUTES PLUS 30 MINUTES CHILLING TIME

These gently spiced biscuits pack a secret punch – popping candy!

INGREDIENTS:

100 g butter, soft

100 g caster sugar

225 g plain flour

½ tsp ground cinnamon

½ tsp ground ginger

1 tsp orange zest

1 egg, beaten

20 g sprinkles

20 g popping candy

30 g dark chocolate chips

EQUIPMENT:

Electric whisk

1. Add the butter and sugar to a large bowl and mix with an electric whisk until the mixture has combined and is a light-yellow colour.
2. Add the flour, cinnamon, ginger and orange zest, and mix.
3. Add the egg and continue to mix until the ingredients start to form a dough.
4. Bring the dough together with your hands. If the dough is sticky, dust your hands with a little flour. If the dough feels too dry, add 1 tbsp of milk.
5. Shape the dough into a log shape, approximately 6 cm thick and 9 cm long.
6. Wrap the log in cling film and put it in the fridge for 30 minutes. Do not skip this step!
7. Preheat the air fryer to 175°C/350°F for 5 minutes.
8. Remove the biscuit dough from the fridge and unwrap it.
9. Use a sharp knife to cut 0.5-cm-thick slices of dough from the log.
10. Place a liner into the air fryer basket.
11. Carefully arrange the slices of biscuit dough on the liner. Try to leave at least 3 cm space around each biscuit. You may need to work in batches.
12. Set the temperature to 175°C/350°F and the timer for 6 minutes.

13 When the time is up, open the fryer. The biscuits should have turned a deeper yellow colour and should look dry on top. They may be a little browner around the edges. If the biscuits look a little raw, close the fryer and cook for another 2–3 minutes before checking again.

14 Carefully remove the biscuits from the fryer using tongs or a spatula and place on a cooling rack.

15 Tip the sprinkles and popping candy into a small bowl and stir well.

16 Tip the chocolate chips into a microwave-safe bowl. Heat the bowl in a microwave for 1 minute. When the time is up, remove the bowl from the microwave and give the chocolate chips a stir. If they have mostly melted with just a few solid ones in the centre, continue to stir until they have all melted. If there are still a lot of solid chocolate chips, put the bowl back in the microwave and heat for another 10 seconds before checking again. Remove the bowl from the microwave, and stir.

17 Dip one biscuit into the chocolate, you can dip half the biscuit or the top side of the whole biscuit. Hold the biscuit over the bowl to let as much excess melted chocolate drip back into the bowl.

18 Place the chocolate-coated biscuit on a piece of greaseproof paper. Add a pinch of the sprinkles onto the melted chocolate. Repeat for the rest of your biscuits.

19 Leave the biscuits in a cool place so the chocolate can set, then serve. These biscuits are best enjoyed on the same day they were made.

STONE-FRUIT CRUMBLES

SERVES 2 | TAKES 20 MINUTES

Juicy roasted peach or nectarine halves topped with a crisp sweet crumble make an ideal early autumn pud.

INGREDIENTS:

- 2 ripe peaches or nectarines
- 2 tbsp brown sugar
- 4 tbsp rolled oats
- 2 tbsp plain flour
- 20 g butter, melted
- 4 tsp chopped nuts
- 1 tsp ground cinnamon

CHEF IT UP!

Plump for plums! Swap the nectarine or peach for two plums. Serve with a drizzle of custard or a big scoop of ice cream.

1. Preheat the air fryer to 175°C/350°F for 5 minutes.
2. Use a sharp knife to carefully cut the peaches or nectarines in half. Use a teaspoon to remove the stone. Place the halves, cut side up into an ovenproof dish.
3. Sprinkle on half the sugar. Use oven gloves to carefully place the dish into the air fryer basket. Set the temperature to 175°C/350°F and the timer for 6 minutes.
4. Add the rest of the sugar to a bowl and add the oats, flour, butter, chopped nuts and cinnamon. Mix the ingredients together with a spoon.
5. When the time is up, open the fryer. The fruit should have darkened in colour and softened. If it hasn't, put it back in for another 2 minutes before checking again.
6. Carefully scoop 1 tbsp of mixture onto each fruit half.
7. Set the temperature to 175°C/350°F and the timer for 4 minutes.
8. When the time is up, open the fryer. The crumble mixture should look crisp and brown and the fruit should look soft. If the fruit crumbles don't look as done as you would like, close the fryer and cook for another 2–3 minutes before checking again.

Warning! This recipe contains nuts. Make sure none of your family or friends have nut allergies before sharing these crumbles with them.

WINTER

TURKEY BURGERS

MAKES 4 BURGERS | TAKES 30 MINUTES

These burgers are so juicy and delicious that you will want to gobble-gobble them down right away!

INGREDIENTS:

500 g minced turkey

½ medium onion, grated

1 tbsp Worcestershire sauce

½ tsp salt

½ tsp ground black pepper

4 burger buns

4 slices brie

4 lettuce leaves

4 tbsp cranberry sauce

EQUIPMENT:

Meat thermometer

CHEF IT UP! Swap out the cheese and gherkin for any toppings that you like.

1. Preheat the air fryer to 200°C/400°F for 5 minutes.
2. Add the turkey, grated onion, Worcestershire sauce, salt and pepper to a large bowl and mix together with a spoon.
3. Divide the mixture into four and shape into balls. Squash the balls into patties.
4. Place a liner into the air fryer basket. Carefully arrange the burger patties on the liner.
5. Set the temperature to 200°C/400°F and the timer for 7 minutes.
6. When the time is up, open the fryer. Carefully flip your burger patties using tongs. Set the temperature to 200°C/400°F and the timer for 7 minutes.
7. When the time is up, open the fryer and push the tip of a thermometer into the centre of one burger. If the temperature reads 74°C/165°F or above, the burger is cooked. If the burger isn't quite ready, cook for another 1–2 minutes before checking again.
8. When the burgers are ready, top each patty with a slice of brie and cook for 1 minute.
9. Put the bottom half of each bun on a plate and place a slice of lettuce on top. When the burgers are done, use tongs to carefully remove the burgers from the fryer and place each one, cheese-side up, on top of the lettuce.
10. Place 1 tbsp of cranberry sauce on top of the cheese and finish with the top half of the bun.

VG

CRANBERRY AND ORANGE STUFFING BALLS

MAKES 8 STUFFING BALLS | TAKES 35 MINUTES

These stuffing balls make the perfect side dish to a roast dinner or can be enjoyed as a delicious vegetarian snack, all by themselves.

INGREDIENTS:

60 g butter

1 medium onion, chopped

50 g celery, chopped

1 egg, beaten

100 ml cold vegetable stock

½ tsp salt

½ tsp ground black pepper

150 g stale bread, cut into 2–3 cm cubes

4 tbsp parsley, chopped

2 tbsp sage, chopped

1 tsp orange zest

30 g dried cranberries

Oil spray

CHEF IT UP!
Try adding nuts and any fruit you prefer to your stuffing mix. Pine nuts work very well with chopped dried apricots.

1. Melt the butter in a small saucepan over a medium heat. When the butter has melted, add the onions and celery and stir them into the melted butter using a wooden spoon or spatula.

2. Cook the onions and celery over a medium heat for 5 minutes or until soft. Stir to make sure they don't stick to the bottom of the pan. If they start to stick or burn, turn down the heat. When they are soft, and the onions have turned see-through, remove the pan from the heat.

3. Add the egg, vegetable stock, salt and pepper to a large bowl and mix together with a spoon. Add the cubes of bread and stir to help the bread to soak up the stock and egg mixture.

4. Add the herbs, orange zest, dried cranberries, onions and celery to the bowl. Stir until they are all combined. The mixture should look sticky.

5. Preheat the air fryer to 180°C/350°F for 5 minutes.

6. Take a handful of the mixture and squash it into a ball. If the mixture is too dry to stick together, add a little more stock. Stir the mixture before trying to make another ball. If the mixture is too sloppy to make a ball, add some more bread and stir before trying to make another ball.

7. When the mixture is the right consistency, use your hands to divide the stuffing and form it into 8 balls. Put the balls on a plate.

8. Spray the air fryer basket with a little oil. Carefully arrange the balls in the basket. Set the temperature to 180°C/350°F and the timer for 8 minutes.

9. When the time is up, open the fryer and carefully turn the stuffing balls using tongs. Set the temperature to 180°C/350°F and the timer for 6 minutes.

10. When the time is up, open the fryer. The stuffing balls should look crisp and brown. If the balls don't look as crisp as you would like. Cook for another 2–3 minutes before checking again.

11. Carefully remove the stuffing balls from the air fryer using tongs.

PARSNIP CHIPS

SERVES 2 | TAKES 20 MINUTES

Normally found alongside a roast, these herby parsnip chips deserve to be enjoyed as a snack, all by themselves.

INGREDIENTS:

500 g parsnips or 4 medium parsnips

1 tbsp olive oil

¼ tsp salt

¼ tsp ground black pepper

½ tsp garlic powder

½ tsp thyme, dried or fresh

CHEF IT UP! Try using different herbs or flavourings. Honey works especially well with parsnips.

1. Peel the parsnips using a peeler.
2. Use a sharp knife and a cutting board to cut off the top and bottom of the parsnips. Throw away these pieces.
3. Cut the parsnips in half lengthways. Place the parsnips cut-side down on the cutting board and cut them into chips approximately 2 cm thick. It doesn't matter how long they are. A mixture of different lengths makes for a more interesting snack!
4. Preheat the air fryer to 190°C/375°F for 5 minutes.
5. Add the olive oil, salt, pepper, garlic powder and thyme to a bowl and stir.
6. Add the parsnip chips and stir until all of the chips are coated in the oil and flavourings.
7. Arrange the parsnips in the air fryer basket. Set the temperature to 190°C/375°F and the timer for 5 minutes.
8. When the time is up, open the fryer and give the basket a shake to move the chips around. Carefully turn over any stubborn chips using tongs.
9. Close the fryer and set the temperature to 190°C/375°F and the timer for 5 minutes.
10. When the time is up, open the fryer. The chips should look crisp and golden. Push a fork into one chip. If it slides in easily, the chips are ready. If the chip is still too firm or they do not look as golden as you would like, cook for 2–3 more minutes before checking again.
11. Carefully remove the chips from the fryer using tongs, and serve while still hot.

SWEET AND SOUR MEATBALLS

MAKES ROUGHLY 16 MEATBALLS | TAKES 35 MINUTES

These take-away inspired meatballs make a memorable midweek dinner.

INGREDIENTS:

500 g minced pork

40 g dried breadcrumbs

2 tbsp ginger, grated

2 cloves garlic, crushed

2 spring onions, chopped

½ tsp salt

½ tsp ground black pepper

Oil spray

FOR THE SAUCE:

1 tbsp cornflour

200 ml pineapple juice

50 ml ketchup

50 g sugar

2 tbsp soy sauce

TO SERVE:

150 g cooked white rice

1. Add the pork, breadcrumbs, ginger, garlic, spring onions, salt and pepper to a large bowl. Mix together using a spoon. You may need to use your hands to bring the mixture together, and make sure it is thoroughly blended.

2. Preheat the air fryer to 180°C/350°F for 5 minutes.

3. Pinch a large ping-pong-ball-sized chunk of mixture and roll it between your palms to make a ball. Place the ball on a large plate. Repeat until all of the mixture has been turned into meatballs.

4. Spray the air fryer basket with a little oil. Use tongs to carefully arrange the meatballs in the basket. Leave a little room around each meatball. You may need to work in batches. Set the temperature to 180°C/350°F and the timer for 8 minutes.

5. Add the cornflour to a cup or small bowl. Add 2 tbsp of the pineapple juice and stir. Put this to one side.

6. Heat a small saucepan over a medium heat. Add the rest of the pineapple juice, ketchup, sugar and soy sauce. Stir together and heat until the mixture starts to boil. Add the cornflour and pineapple-juice mixture and stir again. Lower the heat to a simmer and stir. The sauce should start to thicken. When the sauce is thick enough to coat the back of the spoon, turn down the heat to the lowest level to keep it warm until the meatballs are ready.

WINTER

7 When the time is up, open the fryer. The meatballs should look sizzling and brown. To test whether they are cooked, push the tip of a thermometer into the middle of one meatball. If the temperature reads 62°C/145°F or above, the meatballs are done. If the meatballs are not ready, cook for another 2–3 minutes before checking again.

8 Remove the meatballs from the fryer using tongs and put them in a medium bowl.

9 If you have remaining meatballs, repeat steps 4 to 9 until all the meatballs are cooked.

10 Pour over the sauce and stir until all of the meatballs are coated in the sauce. Serve hot over white rice.

CRISPY SESAME BEEF

SERVES 2 | TAKES 45 MINS PLUS 1–4 HOURS MARINATING TIME

Try making this Asian-inspired dish instead of ordering in.

INGREDIENTS:

1 tbsp soy sauce

½ tbsp sesame oil

1 tbsp sugar

½ tsp garlic powder

½ tsp ground ginger

250 g lean steak, cut into 2-cm-thick strips

3 tbsp cornflour

Oil spray

FOR THE SAUCE:

1 tbsp vegetable oil

½ medium onion, chopped

3 garlic cloves, crushed

1 tbsp grated ginger

1 medium pepper, cut into strips

2 tbsp soy sauce

2 tbsp rice wine vinegar

1 tbsp mild sweet chilli sauce

TO SERVE:

150 g cooked white rice

1 tsp sesame seeds

1 spring onion, chopped

1. Add the soy sauce, sesame oil, sugar, garlic powder and ground ginger to a bowl and mix well with a spoon. Do not add the cornflour just yet.

2. Add the steak strips to the bowl and toss in the mixture until well coated. Cover the bowl with cling film or a plate and put it in the fridge. Leave the bowl in the fridge for 1 to 4 hours. The longer you leave the steak, the more flavour it will absorb.

3. Preheat the air fryer to 200°C/400°F for 5 minutes.

4. Remove the steak from the fridge and uncover the bowl. Add the cornflour. Toss the steak in the cornflour until each strip is covered in the flour-marinade mixture.

5. Remove the strips from the bowl and lay them out on a piece of kitchen roll. Spray each strip with a little oil.

6. Carefully place the strips of beef into the hot air fryer basket using tongs. Try to spread them evenly across the basket.

7	Set the temperature to 200°C/400°F and the timer for 5 minutes.
8	Heat 1 tbsp of oil in a frying pan. When the oil is hot, add the chopped onion, garlic, grated ginger and pepper strips. Use a wooden spoon or spatula to keep the ingredients moving in the pan, to make sure they don't burn.
9	When the onions and pepper start to look a little soft, add the soy sauce, rice wine vinegar and sweet chilli sauce to the pan and stir.
10	Cook the sauce until it starts to bubble. Remove the pan from the heat and put it to one side.
11	When the time is up, open the fryer and carefully turn the strips using tongs. Cook the strips for another 3 minutes.
12	When the time is up, open the fryer. The beef should be sizzling and look crisp. If it is not as cooked as you would like, close the fryer and cook for another 2 minutes before checking again.
13	Carefully remove the strips from the fryer using tongs. Add the strips to the frying pan with the sauce, then stir until the beef strips are coated in the sauce.
14	Serve the beef on top of white rice. Sprinkle the sesame seeds and spring onions onto the beef before serving.

CHEESY ARTICHOKE FONDUE

SERVES 2-4 | TAKES 25 MINUTES

Take your fondue game to the next level with this warm and cheesy vegetable dip.

INGREDIENTS:

200 g tinned artichokes, drained

150 g frozen spinach, thawed

100 g cream cheese

60 g soured cream

50 g mayonnaise

1 clove garlic, crushed or grated

30 g parmesan cheese, grated

30 g mozzarella cheese, grated

30 g gruyère cheese, grated

½ tsp ground black pepper

½ tsp chilli flakes

CHEF IT UP!
Crumble some slices of cooked bacon into your mixture before cooking to give a smoky flavour.

1. Preheat the air fryer to 175°C/350°F for 5 minutes.
2. Use a sharp knife and a cutting board to carefully chop your artichokes into 1–2-cm pieces. They will fall apart a bit, but don't worry. Add the artichokes to a large bowl.
3. Add the rest of the ingredients to the bowl and mix thoroughly with a spoon until they are well combined.
4. Spoon all of the mixture into an ovenproof dish and smooth over the top with the back of a spoon.
5. Carefully put the ovenproof dish into the hot air fryer basket using oven gloves or tongs.
6. Set the temperature to 175°C/350°F and the timer for 10 minutes.
7. When the time is up, open the fryer. The surface of your dip should look golden brown and the mixture should be bubbling underneath. If the dip does not look as well done as you would like, cook for another 2–3 minutes at 175°C/350°F before checking again.
8. Remove the ovenproof dish from the fryer using oven gloves or tongs. The dip will be very hot, so be very careful not to spill it.
9. Serve warm with thin slices of baguette and sticks of your favourite crunchy fresh veggies.

VG

WINTER BERRY BREAKFAST OATS

SERVES 2 | TAKES 20 MINUTES

Use your air fryer to transform a boring bowl of porridge into a protein-packed breakfast oat bake!

INGREDIENTS:

Butter for greasing

40 g rolled oats

1 medium egg

½ banana

3 tbsp milk

¼ tsp baking powder

¼ tsp ground cinnamon

¼ tsp salt

2 tsp honey, plus a little extra for drizzling

1 tbsp dried cranberries

1 tbsp flaked almonds

EQUIPMENT:

2 ramekins, roughly 9 cm x 5 cm or 200 ml capacity

CHEF IT UP! Why not add chocolate chips or even sprinkles to the batter before baking? A scoop of cool Greek yogurt makes an excellent accompaniment.

1. Grease the inside of the ramekins by dipping a piece of kitchen roll in butter and rubbing it around the inside. Make sure each ramekin is completely covered.

2. Preheat the air fryer 150°C/300°F for 5 minutes.

3. Crack the egg into a jug. Add the banana, oats, milk, baking powder, cinnamon, salt and honey.

4. Mix and break up the ingredients using a hand blender. Blend the ingredients until there are no lumps.

5. Add three-quarters of the dried cranberries and three-quarters of the flaked almonds to the blended mixture. Stir with a spoon to combine.

6. Pour the mixture into the greased ramekins. Sprinkle the rest of the cranberries and almonds on top. Cover each ramekin with a piece of foil. Seal the foil by crimping it around the edge of the ramekins.

7. Carefully place the ramekins in the air fryer basket. Set the temperature to 150°C/300°F and the timer for 6 minutes. When the time is up, open the fryer and carefully remove the foil using tongs. Set the temperature to 150°C/300°F and the timer for 8 minutes.

WINTER

8 When the time is up, open the fryer. The top of the oat bakes should look brown and solid, with no wet bits. To check if they are cooked, push the tip of a table knife into the centre of one bake. The blade should come out clean with just a few crumbs. If the blade comes out with raw batter on it, or if the top does not look as brown as you would like, close the fryer and cook for another 1–2 minutes before checking again.

9 Carefully remove the bakes from the fryer using tongs.

10 Serve warm with a drizzle of honey.

STICKY TOFFEE PUDDING

MAKES 4 PUDDINGS | TAKES 40 MINUTES

This super-sticky family favourite dessert makes a wonderfully wintry after-dinner treat.

INGREDIENTS:

80 g pitted dates

120 ml boiling water

100 g flour

1 tsp baking powder

½ tsp bicarbonate of soda

1 tsp ground mixed spice

80 g butter, room temperature, plus a little extra for greasing

80 g brown sugar

1 egg, beaten

2 tbsp golden syrup

FOR THE SAUCE:

100 g butter

80 g brown sugar

150 ml double cream

EQUIPMENT:

4 pudding tins or ramekins, 9 cm x 5 cm or 200 ml capacity

1. Prepare the pudding tins by dipping a piece of kitchen roll into some butter and using it to rub the butter around the inside of the tins. Continue until there is a thin coating of butter inside all four tins.

2. Pour 120 ml of boiling water into a jug and add the dates. Put this to one side.

3. Add the flour, baking powder, bicarbonate of soda and mixed spice to a bowl and mix together. Put this to one side.

4. Add the butter and sugar to a medium bowl and mix together with a wooden spoon. Keep mixing until you have a creamy consistency. You can use an electric mixer if you have one.

5. Add the beaten egg. Continue blending until all the egg is mixed in. Mix in the golden syrup next. Put this to one side.

6. Take the jug with the water and dates and use a hand blender to blend until there are no remaining chunks of date. You can use a food processor for this if you have one. If you do not have either of these, remove the dates from the water and chop them very finely using a sharp knife. Scrape the dates back into the water and stir.

7. Add the date mixture to the wet ingredients and stir together until well combined.

8. Preheat the air fryer to 160°C/320°F for 5 minutes.

9. Add one third of the dry ingredients to the wet ingredients and mix until well combined. Repeat with half of the remaining ingredients. And then again with the rest. Continue to mix until there are no dry ingredients left and the mixture is smooth and creamy.

10. Spoon the mixture into the prepared pudding tins. Divide the mixture evenly between all four tins.

11. Use tongs to carefully place the tins in the air fryer basket. Set the temperature to 160°C/320°F and the timer for 15 minutes.

12. To make the sauce, add the butter and brown sugar to a small saucepan. Heat it over a medium temperature until the butter has melted. Stir the mixture until the sugar has melted into the butter.

13. Add the cream and heat until the mixture starts to bubble. Stir the bubbling mixture for 5 minutes before turning off the heat.

14. When the time is up, the tops of your puddings should look dark brown. To check if they are cooked, insert the blade of a table knife into the centre of one pudding. If the puddings are cooked, the blade will come out clean with a few crumbs clinging to it. If there is raw mixture on it, close the fryer and cook for another 2–3 minutes before checking again.

15. Use tongs to remove the tins from the fryer and place them on a cooling rack.

16. When the puddings are cool enough to touch, remove them from their tins by running a table knife around the edges of the tins and turning them upside down onto a plate. The tins may need a little shake.

17. Once out of their tins, top each pudding with a few large spoonfuls of sauce and serve.

SNOWY FIR TREES

MAKES ROUGHLY 12 MERINGUE TREES | TAKES 1 HOUR 40 MINUTES

What better on a winter's day than a crisp, snowy snack? These meringue trees are delicious served with a cup of steaming hot chocolate.

INGREDIENTS:

2 egg whites

1 tsp cornflour

1 tsp white vinegar

½ tsp vanilla extract

120 g caster sugar

Sprinkles

EQUIPMENT:

Electric whisk

Piping bag

Star nozzle

1. Add the egg whites to a large bowl. Whisk using an electric whisk or stand mixer. The egg whites will get bubblier and bubblier until they form a thick white foam.

2. When the egg whites look thick and foamy and keep their shape, add the cornflour, white vinegar, vanilla extract and one quarter of the sugar. Whisk again until the sugar has mixed in.

3. Add the remaining sugar one quarter at a time and continue to whisk for 3 minutes. The egg whites should end up looking thick and glossy and form stiff peaks when you lift up the whisk.

4. Cut a piece of greaseproof paper to the size of a tray that will fit inside your air fryer. Place the paper on top of the tray.

5. Cut 3 cm off the tip of the piping bag using scissors and insert the star nozzle so that the end of the nozzle pokes out of the bottom. Hold the piping bag in your least dominant hand with the nozzle pointing downwards. Use your other hand to turn the top half of the piping bag inside out, over your hand.

6. Spoon the meringue into the piping bag until it is two-thirds full, folding up the piping bag as it fills. Squeeze the top of the piping bag until meringue starts to come out of the nozzle.

7. To make your trees, hold the nozzle of the piping bag close to the greaseproof paper. Gently squeeze the piping bag until you have piped a star shape about 4 cm across. While still squeezing, push the nozzle into the meringue before pulling it up by a centimetre. Squeeze a second layer slightly smaller than the first. Repeat this to make the top of the tree. To make the pointy tip, push the nozzle into the meringue very slightly and pull it away.

8. Don't worry if your trees look a bit messy, they will still taste delicious! If your piping skills get better as you go, scrape the first trees you made back into the bowl to return to the piping bag when you are ready.

9. Repeat step 7 to make your next tree. Pipe this 2–3 centimetres away from the first one and continue to make trees until you have run out of mixture or the tray is full. You may need to cook the trees in batches.

10. Decorate the trees with a few sprinkles.

11. Place the tray inside the air fryer. Set the temperature to 120°C/250°F and the timer for 20 minutes.

12. When the time is up, set the temperature to 95°C/200°F and the timer for 1 hour.

13. Carefully remove the tray from the fryer using tongs or oven gloves and leave to cool on a heatproof mat or rack.

14. The meringue trees can be stored in an airtight container for 2–3 weeks.

CHEF IT UP!

Practice makes perfect! Practise with your piping bag until you are confident, then see what else you can make. Air fryer pavlova, anyone? Simply top your meringue with whipped cream and your favourite fruit. Delish!

WINTER

VG

PEPPERMINT SWIRLS

MAKES 16–18 BISCUITS | TAKES 30 MINS PLUS 1 HOUR CHILLING TIME

These peppermint biscuits pair perfectly with a glass of milk or even better given as a gift!

INGREDIENTS:

100 g butter, softened

100 g caster sugar

225 g plain flour

1 egg, beaten

4–8 tsp milk

½ tsp vanilla extract

½ tsp peppermint extract

A few drops of red food colouring

EQUIPMENT:

Electric whisk

CHEF IT UP! Do you know what goes very well with mint? Chocolate! Dip each biscuit in a little melted chocolate and leave them to set before serving.

1. Add the butter and sugar to a large bowl and mix with an electric whisk until the mixture is combined. It should look a light-yellow colour.
2. Tip in the flour and continue to mix until well combined.
3. Add the egg and 1 tsp of milk and continue to mix. Keep adding the milk 1 tsp at a time until the ingredients start to form a dough. You may not need to add all of the milk.
4. Divide the mixture into two equal portions and transfer one half to a second large bowl. Put one bowl to the side.
5. Add the vanilla extract to the first bowl and bring the dough together with your hands. If the dough is sticky, dust your hands with a little flour. If the dough feels too dry, add a few drops of extra milk.
6. Add the peppermint extract and a few drops of red food colouring to the dough in the second bowl. Mix using the electric whisk until well combined. If the dough does not look as red as you would like, add a few more drops of red food colouring and mix again.
7. Bring the dough together using your hands, and then put the bowl to one side.
8. Sprinkle a little flour onto a clean work surface and place the vanilla dough on top. Sprinkle the top of the dough with a little more flour.
9. Use a rolling pin to roll out your dough into a rectangle measuring approximately 18 x 25 cm.
10. Repeat steps 8 and 9 with the red peppermint dough.
11. Place the red peppermint dough on top of the vanilla dough. Roll the rolling pin over the top of the two sheets of dough to help stick them together. Use a table knife to tidy up the edges of the rectangle.

12. Work from one of the long edges and start rolling the two doughs together using your hands. Aim to create a long log shape with a tight spiral.

13. Wrap the log of dough in cling film and chill it in the fridge for 1 hour. Do not skip this step.

14. Preheat the air fryer to 160°C/325°F for 5 minutes.

15. Remove the biscuit dough from the fridge and unwrap it.

16. Use a sharp knife to cut 1.5-cm-thick slices of dough from the log. Place each slice on a clean work surface, then use a rolling pin to roll out each slice until it is 1 cm thick. This will help the swirl stay together.

17. Place a liner into the air fryer basket.

18. Use tongs or a spatula to carefully place the slices of biscuit dough onto the liner. Try to leave at least 3 cm around each biscuit. You may need to work in batches.

19. Set the temperature to 160°C/325°F and the timer for 7 minutes.

20. When the time is up, open the fryer. The biscuits should have turned a deeper colour and look dry on top. They may be a little browner around the edges. If the biscuits look a little raw, close the fryer and cook for another 2–3 minutes before checking again.

21. Carefully remove the biscuits from the fryer using tongs or a spatula and place onto a cooling rack.

FESTIVE PASTIES

MAKES 10 MINI PASTIES | TAKES 25 MINUTES

A tasty twist on a Christmas classic. You are bound to have to make more than one batch of these over the festive season.

INGREDIENTS:

1 tbsp plain flour

350 g shortcrust pastry

200 g mincemeat

1 egg

EQUIPMENT:

10 cm pastry cutter

Pastry brush

CHEF IT UP!
These mini pies don't just have to be for Christmas. Why not try making mini pasties filled with your favourite jam or marmalade? Delish!

1. Sprinkle half the flour onto a clean work surface. Place the pastry on top. Sprinkle the rest of the flour on top of the pastry and smooth it over the surface so that it is covered in a light dusting.

2. Use a rolling pin to roll out the pastry until it is approximately 3 mm thick.

3. Use a 10-cm cutter to press circles out of the pastry. Press out as many as you can and put them to one side.

4. Gather up the rest of the pastry and roll it out again until is 3 mm thick, then press out more circles. Keep going until you do not have enough pastry left to roll out another circle.

5. Brush a little water around the rim of each circle. Put 1 tsp of mincemeat in the centre of each circle. Do not add too much or the pasties will not close.

6. Fold the pastry over the mincemeat to make a small pasty. Press the top edge into the bottom to seal. Use the back of a fork to crimp the round edge of each pasty.

7. Push the prongs of the fork into the centre of each pasty to make small holes. These holes will allow steam to escape while the pasties are cooking.

8. Repeat steps 5–7 for each circle of pastry.

9. Preheat the air fryer to 180°C/360°F for 5 minutes.

10. Use a pastry brush to brush the pasties with a little beaten egg.

11. Carefully place a liner into the air fryer basket. Carefully arrange the pasties on top of the liner. Try to leave a bit of space around each pasty. You may need to work in batches.

12. Set the temperature to 180°C/360°F and the timer for 5 minutes.

13. When the time is up, open the fryer. Carefully turn the pasties over using tongs, and cook for another 3 minutes at 180°C/360°F.

14. When the time is up, open the fryer. The pasties should look crisp and golden. If they do not look as crisp as you would like, cook for another 2 minutes before checking again.

15. Carefully remove the pasties from the fryer using tongs and place them on a cooling rack. Let them cool down for at least 5 minutes before eating, they will be very hot inside!

INDEX

Air Fried Alaska 52
air frying
    advantages of 4
    cooking tips 5
    equipment 6
    safety tips................................ 5
    types of fryers 4
Avocado Dippers 36-7

Baklava Parcels 20-1
beef: Crispy Sesame Beef........ 82-3
biscuits and cakes
    Carrot Cupcakes...............18-19
    Easter Egg Cookies 26
    Firecracker Biscuits 70-1
    Parkin Mini Loaf..................... 65
    Peppermint Swirls 92-3
    Red Velvet Cupcakes 22-3
    Spiced Apple Cake 66-7
    Spring Green Matcha Biscuits.... 64
    Strawberry and Cream Butterfly
    Cakes 48-9
bread
    Chocolate Orange Bread Puddings.
    24-5
    Cranberry and Orange Stuffing
    Balls 76-7
    Falafel Pitta Pockets 40-1
    Jammy French Toast Rollups ... 50-1
    Spring Onion Soda Bread.... 12-13
    Super-Simple Flat Breads 29
    Welsh Rarebit 9

Caramelized Pineapple 46
Carrot Cupcakes................... 18-19
Cauliflower Steak, Roasted........ 44-5
cheese
    Cheese Mummies..................... 59
    Cheesy Artichoke Fondue....... 84-5
    Halloumi Mini Skewers 34-5
    Herby Hot Potato Salad 28
    Jammy French Toast Rollups ... 50-1
    Welsh Rarebit 9
chicken
    Chicken Tikka Bites 56-7
    Hot Honey Chicken Strips 30-1
chocolate
    Chocolate Chip Catherine Wheels..
    68-9
    Chocolate Marshmallow Fondue
    with Mini Fruit Skewers 47
    Chocolate Orange Bread Puddings.
    24-5
    Firecracker Biscuits 70-1
Cranberry and Orange Stuffing Balls
.... 76-7
Crispy 'Crab' Snacks 33
Crispy Sesame Beef 82-3
desserts

    Air Fried Alaska 52
    Baklava Parcels 20-1
    Caramelized Pineapple 46
    Chocolate Marshmallow Fondue
    with Mini Fruit Skewers 47
    Chocolate Orange Bread Puddings.
    24-5
    Snowy Fir Trees 90-1
    Sticky Toffee Pudding 88-9
    Stone Fruit Crumbles 72

eggs
    Egg Blossoms 8
    Ham and Cheese Quiche 38-9
    Scotch Eggs 10-11
    Snowy Fir Trees 90-1

Falafel Pitta Pockets 40-1
Festive Pasties 94-5
Firecracker Biscuits 70-1
fish and seafood
    Crispy 'Crab' Snacks 33
    Prawn Scampi 32
    Smoked Salmon Loaded Potato Skins
    14-15
fruit
    Caramelized Pineapple 46
    Chocolate Marshmallow Fondue
    with Mini Fruit Skewers 47
    Cranberry and Orange Stuffing
    Balls 76-7
    Spiced Apple Cake 66-7
    Stone Fruit Crumbles 72
    Strawberry and Cream Butterfly
    Cakes 48-9
    Winterberry Breakfast Oats.... 86-7

Garlic Stuffed Mushrooms........ 60-1

Halloumi Mini Skewers 34-5
Ham and Cheese Quiche 38-9
Herby Hot Potato Salad 28
Hot Honey Chicken Strips 30-1

Jammy French Toast Rollups 50-1

Lamb Shish Kebabs................ 42-3

Masala Spiced Mixed Nuts 58
Mushrooms, Garlic Stuffed........ 60-1

nuts
    Baklava Parcels 20-1
    Masala Spiced Mixed Nuts 58
    Pumpkin Spiced Granola 62-3
    Stone Fruit Crumbles 72

oats
    Pumpkin Spiced Granola 62-3

Stone Fruit Crumbles 72
Winterberry Breakfast Oats.... 86-7

Pakora, Vegetable 16-17
Parkin Mini Loaf 65
Parsnip Chips........................ 78-9
pastry
    Baklava Parcels 20-1
    Cheese Mummies................... 59
    Chocolate Chip Catherine Wheels..
    68-9
    Festive Pasties 94-5
Peppermint Swirls 92-3
Pineapple, Caramelized 46
pork: Sweet and Sour Meatballs ......
.... 80-1
Prawn Scampi 32
Pumpkin Soup 54-5
Pumpkin Spiced Granola 62-3

Red Velvet Cupcakes 22-3
Roasted Cauliflower Steak...... 44-5

Scotch Eggs 10-11
skewers and kebabs
    Chicken Tikka Bites 56-7
    Chocolate Marshmallow Fondue
    with Mini Fruit Skewers 47
    Halloumi Mini Skewers 34-5
    Lamb Shish Kebabs................ 42-3
    Smoked Salmon Loaded Potato Skins
    14-15
Snowy Fir Trees 90-1
soups: Pumpkin Soup 54-5
Spiced Apple Cake 66-7
Spring Green Matcha Biscuits...... 64
Spring Onion Soda Bread...... 12-13
Sticky Toffee Pudding 88-9
Stone Fruit Crumbles 72
Sweet and Sour Meatballs........ 80-1

Turkey Burgers 74-5

vegetables
    Avocado Dippers.................. 36-7
    Cheesy Artichoke Fondue....... 84-5
    Egg Blossoms 8
    Falafel Pitta Pockets 40-1
    Garlic Stuffed Mushrooms......... 60
    Halloumi Mini Skewers 34-5
    Herby Hot Potato Salad 28
    Parsnip Chips........................ 78-9
    Pumpkin Soup 54-5
    Roasted Cauliflower Steak...... 44-5
    Vegetable Pakora 16-17

Winterberry Breakfast Oats 86-7